THE ULTIMATE SENIOR TRAVEL GUIDE

Tailored and Practical Advice, Inspiration for New Adventures, Comprehensive Planning Tools, and Enhanced Travel Experience

---

PAULINE WINSLOW

Contents

Introduction 9

1. SETTING THE STAGE FOR SENIOR TRAVEL 13
   Rediscovering the Joy of Travel in Your Golden Years 13
   Overcoming the Fear of Starting Late 15
   The Art of Slow Travel: Savoring Each Moment 18

2. NAVIGATING THE DIGITAL AGE OF TRAVEL 21
   Smartphones and Apps: The Senior Traveler's Toolkit 21
   Online Security Basics for Booking and Browsing 24
   Social Media for Sharing and Inspiration 26

3. PLANNING YOUR JOURNEY 29
   Destinations that Resonate with Senior Travelers 29
   Budgeting for Your Dream Vacation 32
   Travel Insurance: Navigating Your Needs and Options 34

4. SOLO AND GROUP DYNAMICS 37
   The Liberating Experience of Solo Travel 37
   Group Travel: Finding Your Tribe and Traveling Together 40
   Combining Solo and Group Travel 42

5. HEALTH AND SAFETY FIRST — 47
   - Staying Healthy on the Road — 47
   - Safety Tips: Avoiding Common Pitfalls — 50
   - Managing Medications and Health Conditions Abroad — 52

6. SPECIAL INTEREST AND HOBBY-BASED TRAVEL — 57
   - Culinary Tours: A Taste of the World — 57
   - Exploring the Great Outdoors: Bird Watching and Nature Hikes — 60
   - Art and Culture Immersion — 62

7. HIDDEN GEMS ACROSS THE GLOBE — 67
   - The Quiet Charms of Eastern Europe — 67
   - Southeast Asia's Untouched Paradises — 70
   - Exploring the Natural Beauty of South America — 73

8. AMERICAN TREASURES — 77
   - National Parks Through a Senior's Lens — 78
   - Coastal Retreats for Relaxation — 80
   - Cultural Deep Dives in America's Historic Cities — 82

9. CITY BREAKS AND RURAL ESCAPES — 89
   - European Cities with a Slow Pace — 89
   - Rural Retreats in New Zealand and Australia — 91
   - The Allure of Asian Metropolises — 94

10. ACTIVE ADVENTURES AND WELLNESS — 97
    - Walking Tours Tailored for Seniors — 97
    - Yoga Retreats and Wellness Sanctuaries Worldwide — 100
    - Cycling Tours for Every Level of Experience — 102

11. CULTURAL IMMERSION AND
    EDUCATIONAL JOURNEYS   105
    Language Learning Holidays   105
    Volunteer Opportunities Abroad: Giving Back
    While Traveling   108
    Cooking Classes and Wine-Tasting Tours   110

12. DOCUMENTING YOUR TRAVELS   113
    Travel Photography Tips   113
    Keeping a Travel Journal: Capturing Memories
    in Words   116
    Blogging Your Journey: Sharing Stories with
    Loved Ones   118

13. PACKING LIKE A PRO   121
    Essentials for Every Senior Traveler's Suitcase   121
    Gadgets and Gear: Making Travel Comfortable   124
    Toiletries and Medication Checklist   126

14. NAVIGATING AIRPORTS AND PUBLIC
    TRANSPORT   129
    Airport Navigation Tips   129
    Mastering Public Transportation Abroad   132
    Renting a Car Abroad   134

15. BUDGET-FRIENDLY TRAVEL HACKS   137
    Finding the Best Deals on Flights and
    Accommodations   137
    Enjoying Luxury Experiences on a Budget   140
    Free and Low-Cost Attractions Worth Visiting   142

16. BUILDING A COMMUNITY OF SENIOR
    TRAVELERS   147
    Joining Travel Groups and Clubs for Seniors   147
    Sharing Your Travel Experiences   150
    Planning Your Next Adventure   153

Conclusion 157
References 163

© **Copyright Pauline Winslow 2024 - All rights reserved.**

The content within this book may not be reproduced, duplicated or transmitted without direct written permission from the author or the publisher.

Under no circumstances will any blame or legal responsibility be held against the publisher or author for any damages, reparation, or monetary loss due to the information contained within this book. Either directly or indirectly. You are responsible for your own choices, actions, and results.

Legal Notice:

This book is copyright-protected and only for personal use. You cannot amend, distribute, sell, use, quote, or paraphrase any part of the content without the consent of the author or publisher.

Disclaimer Notice:

Please note that the information in this document is for educational and entertainment purposes only. All effort has been expended to present accurate, up-to-date, reliable, and complete information. No warranties of any kind are declared or implied. Readers acknowledge that the author does not render legal, financial, medical, or professional advice. The content within this book has been derived from various sources. Please consult a licensed professional before attempting any techniques outlined in this book.

By reading this document, the reader agrees that the author is under no circumstances responsible for any direct or indirect losses incurred from using the information contained within this document, including, but not limited to, errors, omissions, or inaccuracies.

Introduction

Have you ever stood at the edge of a historic plaza, the morning sun casting long shadows over cobblestones worn smooth by centuries, and felt the weight of ages lift off your shoulders? Travel, especially in the later chapters of life, is not just a change in scenery but a gateway to rejuvenate the spirit, challenge the body, and enrich the mind. This isn't just about seeing new places; it's about transforming how we see ourselves and our world.

As someone who has spent years weaving the art of travel into practical strands of advice for all ages, my passion finds a special echo in helping those in their golden years. I understand the hurdles and the hesitations that might cloud your enthusiasm —health concerns, safety worries, budget constraints, and the daunting prospect of navigating foreign environments. This book is my heartfelt response to those concerns, crafted to turn them from barriers into stepping stones.

"The Ultimate Senior Travel Guide" is more than a travel book. It is a compass for rediscovering joy and adventure at a time in life when each moment counts doubly. It seeks to arm you with the confidence to explore and the practical know-how to do so smoothly and safely.

Travel offers immense benefits, including staying active, engaging with new cultures, and meeting people from all walks of life. Studies have shown that traveling can improve seniors' cognitive health and emotional well-being. This book taps into those benefits, guiding you through adapting travel plans to fit your pace and preferences.

Structured to be your travel companion, the book covers various topics, from choosing the right destinations to understanding the nitty-gritty of travel insurance. You'll find chapters dedicated to budget-friendly travel, managing health on the road, and even how to document your journeys to share with loved ones. Each section blends detailed advice with inspiring stories and practical tips, such as leveraging technology for easier travel planning.

I speak directly to you—whether you're planning a solo adventure, setting off with your partner, or considering a group journey. Each page respects your unique path and offers tailored advice to enhance your travel experience. For instance, you'll find anecdotes that resonate with the spirit of senior adventurers, coupled with quotes that motivate and provoke thought.

Moreover, this book includes interactive elements designed to make planning as enjoyable as the journey. From QR codes linking to online resources to checklists ensuring you've got everything covered, these tools simplify your travel process.

As you turn these pages, I encourage you to dream about the destinations within and use the steps and stories here as a springboard into your next great adventure. Embrace the unknown with enthusiasm and the assurance that you have a knowledgeable friend in these pages.

I am thrilled about the journey you are about to undertake and confident that this guide will become an indispensable part of your travel toolkit. Let's explore the amazing world together with curiosity and confidence. Happy travels!

ONE

Setting the Stage for Senior Travel

Do you recall the exhilarating rush of freedom when you first learned to ride a bike? That wind-in-your-hair, wide-open-road feeling is not just for the young or the restless—it's also perfectly suited for those of us enjoying the silver streaks of seniority. Travel after retirement isn't about ticking boxes or filling photo albums; it's about reawakening that glorious sense of adventure and curiosity tempered with the wisdom of life experience and the luxury of time. Let's dust off the suitcases and tweak the itineraries because the world is waiting, and it's got senior discounts.

Rediscovering the Joy of Travel in Your Golden Years

The moment you retire, it's as if the universe hands you a key to new realms. Travel, especially now, can be infused with leisure and exploration at a pace that sings harmoniously with your own. Gone are the days of squeezing adventures into two-week windows or coordinating with the chaotic schedules of the working world. Imagine strolling through the lavender fields of Provence on a Tuesday morning or exploring the ancient temples of Cambodia on a Thursday afternoon. This newfound freedom means you can avoid the weekend crowds and high season prices, making travel more enjoyable and gentler on the pension.

Tailoring your voyages to your passions and interests is one of the true joys of senior travel. Whether you've always been fascinated by the intricate art of Japanese tea ceremonies or have a budding interest in bird photography, thanks to the new feeder in your backyard, this phase of life allows you to dive deep into these pursuits. Travel becomes more than just visiting a place; it transforms into learning experiences that resonate with your hobbies and lifelong interests. It's about choosing destinations that spark a light in your eyes—be it from the history-soaked cobblestone streets of Rome or the wild, natural beauty of the Scottish Highlands.

Now, let's talk about the physical perks of staying active. Who said retirement means slowing down? If anything, it's the perfect time to lace up those walking shoes and hit the trails of the national parks or even the pavements of new cities. Walking tours, swimming in the clear seas of the Greek islands, or even chasing your grandkids around the playgrounds of Central Park —these activities aren't just good for the body; they keep the heart young and the spirits high. Regular physical activity, as recommended by health professionals, is pivotal in managing symptoms of arthritis, heart disease, and even depression—common concerns as we age.

Mental and emotional well-being is another treasure trove that travel helps unlock. New experiences are like brain food, nourishing our neurons with stimulation and novelty. Every new landscape or culture encountered is a mini workout for the brain, combating the mundanity that sometimes colors our daily routines. Beyond the biological benefits, the joy of discovery, the thrill of meeting new people, and the pride of navigating a foreign city can significantly boost your mood and outlook on life. Plus, let's face it, sharing stories of your escapades at the next family gathering or book club meeting is always a bonus, isn't it?

Reflective Journaling Prompt

Why not start a travel journal to make this journey even more meaningful? Here's a prompt to get you started: Write about a place you visited that left a lasting impression on you. What was it about the location that moved you? Was it the people, the landscapes, or perhaps the local cuisine? Reflecting on these experiences can deepen your appreciation and offer insights into what you'd like your next adventure to involve.

Overcoming the Fear of Starting Late

So, you're looking at your suitcase, maybe dusting off that old passport, and a thought niggles at the back of your mind: "Am I too late to start traveling?" Let me tell you, the starting gun hasn't gone off yet; you're just in time for a different kind of race. It is one where the pace is set by pleasure, not pressure, and unforgettable experiences replace the finish line. However, feeling apprehensive about entering unfamiliar territories is normal, especially if travel brochures seem dominated by the spry and adventurous youth. But here's the secret: travel doesn't have an age limit, and your fears are just undiscovered adventures waiting to be named.

Addressing the common fears of safety, health, and navigation isn't just about offering reassurance. It's about building a toolkit that transforms anxiety into anticipation. Safety is a big concern, and rightfully so. The world can be a daunting place, but there are practical steps you can take to protect yourself. Always check the political stability of a destination before booking your trip, register with your embassy if traveling abroad, and always have access to emergency numbers. Health worries are also a significant barrier. Speak to your doctor before traveling, ensure you have adequate health insurance that covers you internationally, and always carry a list of your medications and allergies in your wallet.

Perhaps the most intimidating aspect is the fear of getting lost in a new city where the signs don't make sense and the language sounds like it's from another planet. Here, technology is your friend. Modern smartphones can be your compass, guidebook, and translator. Before you go, familiarize yourself with helpful apps like Google Maps and Duolingo to brush up on local phrases or TripIt to keep your itinerary organized and at your fingertips.

Building travel confidence doesn't happen overnight. It's like dipping your toes in the ocean before wading in. Start with day trips to nearby towns or attractions. Get used to planning outings, packing an essentials bag, and navigating new places on your own or with a companion. These mini-adventures can significantly boost your confidence, making the idea of longer trips less daunting. Once you're comfortable, extend your range—a weekend stay in a neighboring state, a week-long retreat at a national park, or even a month-long visit to a new country. Each successful trip is a stepping stone to a bigger adventure.

Leveraging your existing social networks can also ease the transition into travel. Let's face it: everything's more fun with friends or even more reassuring. Traveling with companions can not only provide shared joy but also shared support. But what if your friends are all booked up? This is where travel communities come in handy. Numerous online forums and local clubs are brimming with people sharing your travel aspirations. They can offer advice, share experiences, and even provide trip companionship. Websites like Meetup or the AARP travel forums are great places to connect with other senior travelers.

Let's discuss preparation because every good adventure starts with a solid plan. Here's a quick checklist to get you started on the right foot:

1. **Health Check-Up**: Always consult your healthcare provider before embarking on a trip, especially if you have existing conditions.
2. **Travel Insurance**: Opt for insurance that covers medical issues abroad and trip cancellations. It's your safety net, so make sure it's sturdy.
3. **Pack Smart**: Essentials include medications, comfortable shoes, weather-appropriate clothing, copies of your passport, and a basic first-aid kit.
4. **Emergency Information**: Keep a list of emergency contacts, both personal and for your destination, readily accessible.

By tackling these preparatory steps, you ensure a smoother trip and arm yourself against the anxieties that might otherwise hold you back. Remember, the goal isn't just to travel but to transform the journey into a joyous, enriching experience that expands your world in ways you've only imagined. Whether it's the streets of Paris or the trails of Patagonia that call to you, know that it's never too late to answer. So, take that first step because the best moments in life might just be a 'yes' away.

The Art of Slow Travel: Savoring Each Moment

Imagine wandering through a small, sun-dappled Italian village, where every narrow alley tells a story, and every face in the bustling local market is a friendly invitation to conversation. This is slow travel: a way to soak in the world around you at a pace that lets you relish each experience and connect deeply with the place and its people. It's not about checking off a list of attractions; it's about immersing yourself in the essence of a locale, finding joy in the overlooked nooks and crannies that standard tourism often misses.

Slow travel aligns beautifully with the rhythms of senior life, where the rush to climb career ladders or shuttle kids to weekend sports has given way to more measured, thoughtful periods of engagement. For seniors, luxury is in the details—the leisurely morning coffees on a balcony overlooking the Seine or the afternoons spent wandering through a museum, guided by curiosity rather than the ticking clock. This travel style reduces stress and enhances your understanding of diverse cultures and environments. It allows for an authentic experience, encouraging exchanges beyond the superficial and fostering connections that resonate personally.

Slow travel means staying longer in one place rather than hopping from city to city. It might involve renting an apartment or holiday home for several weeks in a quaint

Cornish village or a vibrant Spanish barrio. This gives you a chance to unpack and settle in and offers a taste of local life that is impossible to grasp in a few days. Shopping at neighborhood markets, cooking with local ingredients, and frequenting community cafes enrich your travel experience and contribute to the local economy more meaningfully than typical tourism.

Transport is another element where slow travel can significantly enhance your experience. Instead of stressful airport dashes, consider more scenic, relaxing options like river cruises down the Danube or train journeys across the picturesque landscapes of New Zealand. These modes of travel provide not just comfort but a panorama of changing landscapes and a chance to engage with fellow travelers and locals in a way that air travel seldom permits.

Now, let me share a story that perfectly captures the essence of slow travel. A couple I know, Helen and John, retired last year and decided to spend three months living in a small coastal town in Portugal. They rented a little house by the sea, learned basic Portuguese, and quickly became part of the community. They attended local music nights, participated in a weekly art class, and volunteered at a nearby school. Their experience was so profound that they extended their stay and made lifelong friends. Helen told me this adventure gave them a new perspective on life and a deeper appreciation for different cultures and histories. They lived not as tourists but as locals, and the depth of their experience was infinitely richer for it.

In embracing slow travel, you allow yourself the time to explore, reflect, and absorb—turning what could be a simple trip into a truly transformative experience. It's about quality, not quantity. It's about collecting moments, not just photos. And it's about making each of those moments count, making them rich with learning, laughter, and love. As you plan your next getaway, consider taking it slow. Who knows what wonderful insights and experiences await you when you take the time to stop and smell the roses—or the rosé if you find yourself in a delightful French vineyard.

TWO

Navigating the Digital Age of Travel

Ah, technology! Remember when the height of sophistication was a rotary phone or when getting lost meant unfolding a giant map in the middle of the highway? Times have certainly changed, and while today's gadgets and gizmos might seem overwhelming, they've become invaluable travel companions. So, whether you're a tech-savvy silver surfer or someone who still pines for the simplicity of a dial-up connection, this chapter is about helping you master the digital tools that can transform your travel experiences from good to great.

Smartphones and Apps: The Senior Traveler's Toolkit

Let's dive into the digital toolkit, starting with that mini-computer you carry around in your pocket — the smartphone. Your navigator, translator, tour guide, and personal assistant are all rolled into one compact package. Navigating through apps might feel like wading through a digital jungle, but fear not! I'm here to guide you through some of the most useful travel apps that are as easy to use as they are helpful.

Starting with navigation, apps like Google Maps and Waze are absolute lifesavers for finding your way around. They offer real-time directions, traffic updates, and nearby restaurants or attractions suggestions. Next up, translation apps. Google Translate or Duolingo can help you break down language barriers. Just type in or say what you need to translate, and voilà, you'll be ordering that 'café con leche' like a local in no time!

Thanks to apps like Airbnb and Booking.com, booking accommodations has never been more challenging. With a few taps, you can filter options based on your preferences, browse through photos, and secure a cozy spot for your stay. For exploring local attractions, TripAdvisor and Yelp can be your go-to resources for reviews and recommendations, ensuring you find the best experiences around.

Now, staying connected while traveling is crucial for sharing those enviable photos and for safety and convenience. With messaging apps like WhatsApp and Facebook Messenger, you can easily keep in touch with family and friends back home, share your location, or even make video calls to show off your adventures in real-time. These apps also work on Wi-Fi, which can be a cost-effective way to communicate internationally.

Managing your data and personal information while on the move is equally important. It's all fun and games until someone receives a jaw-dropping roaming bill! To avoid such unpleasant surprises, consider switching to a local SIM card or a global roaming plan that offers affordable rates. Also, be mindful of the Wi-Fi networks you connect to. Public Wi-Fi can be a hacker's playground. Using a Virtual Private Network (VPN) app can help secure your internet connection and protect your data from prying eyes.

But what if all this tech talk sounds like gibberish? Fear not. There are plenty of resources to help you get up to speed. Many community centers offer classes on using smartphones and apps tailored to seniors. They provide a great space to learn and ask questions in a friendly environment.

Additionally, don't underestimate the willingness of younger family members to help. A grandchild's quick tutorial can make a difference in demystifying your device. Plus, it's a wonderful way to spend time together and share something they're proficient in.

Tech Tutorial Resource

For those who prefer to learn at their own pace, YouTube is a treasure trove of tutorial videos ranging from setting up your smartphone to advanced tips on securing your data. Channels like Techboomers or Senior Tech Lessons specifically cater to mature users, making technology approachable and applicable.

Navigating through the digital aspects of travel doesn't have to be a solo journey. With the right tools and a bit of learning, you'll enhance your travel experience and maintain a wonderful connection with your loved ones, sharing every step of your adventure with ease and security. So, embracing the digital age is your ticket to a smoother and more enjoyable travel experience.

Online Security Basics for Booking and Browsing

So, you're ready to use the web to enhance your travels, but let's take a moment—it's a big place and can be tricky to navigate! Navigating the internet securely is crucial, especially when your hard-earned vacation funds and personal info are at stake. Let's talk about how you can safeguard your online activities, ensuring that booking flights and shopping for those snazzy new sandals for the beach is as safe as sipping tea on your porch.

First things first—securing your transactions. Always ensure you're on a secure connection when booking flights or purchasing online. Look for URLs that start with "https" rather than just "http." That extra "s" stands for 'secure'—it's like the safety belt of web browsing. You should also see a little padlock icon near the website address, which tells you the site uses encryption to protect your data. Another good rule of thumb is to use credit cards over debit cards. Credit cards often offer better fraud protection, keeping your bank funds safer. And hey, accumulating those travel rewards points is a nifty bonus, isn't it?

Now, let's go on to guarding your precious personal info. Strong passwords are your first defense—think of them as the sturdy locks on your doors. A strong password should be a mix of letters (both upper and lower case), numbers, and symbols, and please, let's not use "123456" or "password" (you'd be surprised how common that still is!). Consider using a password manager to keep track of all your different passwords; it's like having a personal assistant who's good at keeping secrets. Also, be wary of public Wi-Fi when making transactions or accessing sensitive information. It's too easy for a hacker to sneak a peek through unsecured Wi-Fi networks if you need to access important info while on public Wi-Fi. Use a Virtual Private Network (VPN) to encrypt your data, making it harder for cyber snoops to intercept.

Identifying and sticking to trusted websites can save you a lot of headaches. For travel bookings, stick to well-known, reputable sites like Expedia, Travelocity, or direct airline and hotel websites. Be cautious of offers that seem too good to be true (like those pop-up ads for unbelievable flight deals for $99 to Hawaii). When in doubt, quickly searching for reviews and feedback about the site can help you avoid falling for a scam. For reviews, TripAdvisor and Google Reviews are your go-to resources; they have robust systems to weed out fake reviews and provide a broad spectrum of traveler opinions.

Lastly, let's talk about digital backups. Imagine you're in the beautiful winding streets of Barcelona, and—oops! —you've left your travel documents in your other bag, or worse, they're stolen. Having digital backups of your passport, ID, travel insurance policies, and booking confirmations can be a real trip saver. Use a secure cloud storage service to keep copies of these important documents. Apps like Dropbox or Google Drive offer free storage solutions you can access from anywhere, giving you peace of mind knowing that your essential documents are just a few clicks away, no matter where you are.

Navigating the internet doesn't have to feel like walking a tightrope over a digital abyss. With these simple precautions, you can secure your online transactions, protect your personal information, and enjoy hassle-free preparation for your next great adventure. Remember, the internet is a tool that, when used wisely, can enhance your travel experiences remarkably, making planning and booking as breezy as a beach day in Cancun.

Social Media for Sharing and Inspiration

Ah, social media, the town square of the 21st century! It's where news is broken and lives are shared, and, yes, vacation photos make friends green with envy. If you think social media is only for the young, think again! Platforms like Facebook, Instagram, and Pinterest are fantastic tools for senior travelers like us, not just to brag about our escapades but to connect and draw inspiration for that next getaway.

Think of Facebook as a global coffee shop. You can join various travel groups where members post travel tips, photos, and stories. It's like having a travel magazine that's alive and interactive! You might find yourself scrolling through a post about the best gelato in Rome or a hidden hiking trail in the Rockies. And when it's your turn, sharing your experiences can be just as rewarding. The joy of receiving comments and likes from friends and strangers alike can add an extra layer of enjoyment to your travels.

Instagram, on the other hand, is your digital postcard. It's all about the visuals - stunning sunsets, plates of colorful food, and those 'feet in the sand' pictures that make people wish they were there. But it's not just for showing off those dreamy moments. It's a superb source of inspiration. Want to see the Northern Lights? A quick search for #NorthernLights brings up thousands of breathtaking images and first-hand accounts of this natural spectacle. Plus, you can follow travel influencers who often have tips and insights you won't find in your average travel guide.

Then there's Pinterest, a tool as useful as a Swiss Army knife for travelers—planning a trip to Paris? You can create a board where you pin everything from travel tips to packing lists to the must-visit cafés. It's like crafting your personalized travel brochure, one pin at a time. Moreover, Pinterest is less about social networking and more about gathering ideas, making it a quieter but no less valuable resource.

Navigating privacy settings on these platforms is crucial because while sharing is caring, it's also about maintaining control over online personal space. Each platform has its own settings, and taking the time to understand them is well worth it. For instance, on Facebook, you can customize who sees your posts —from everyone on the internet to just your close family. Consider a private account on Instagram where only approved followers can see your adventures. This way, you keep the memories public for friends but private from prying eyes.

Connecting with communities and like-minded souls across these platforms can significantly enrich your travel experience. Groups and pages are dedicated to senior travel, solo travel, and just about any travel niche you can imagine. Engaging in these communities by asking questions, offering advice, or simply sharing your journey can enhance your travel knowledge and expand your social circle.

Creating engaging content is also a fun aspect of using social media. When capturing photos, try to tell a story with your picture. It could be the bustling chaos of a street market or a serene sunrise from a mountain summit. Remember, the best photos evoke emotion. And when it comes to writing captions, a little humor goes a long way! Share where you are, your thoughts, or how the place made you feel. Did that street performer in Barcelona remind you of your first dance at your wedding? Tell that story!

With its flurry of updates and streams of images, social media might seem daunting at first glance. But with some practice, it's not just manageable; it's enjoyable. It transforms personal adventures into shared experiences, keeps you connected with friends and family, and serves as a wonderful archive of your travels. More than just platforms, Facebook, Instagram, and Pinterest can become your travel journals, your inspiration boards, and part of your journey in the digital age.

Moving from the digital tools that enhance our travel experiences, the next chapter will explore how to ensure those experiences are as smooth and enjoyable as possible. We'll dive into smart travel strategies, from choosing the right accommodations to navigating unexpected hiccups on the road. Stay tuned because the adventure is just getting started!

THREE

Planning Your Journey

Imagine you're sifting through a box of old postcards, each stamped and dusty with tales from places whose names alone—Zanzibar, Timbuktu, Kyoto—whisper hints of adventures. Similarly, each chapter in your travel story begins with a choice of destination. And not just any place off the map, but one that sings to your soul, fits your step and respects your rhythm. This isn't merely choosing where to go; it's about discovering places that resonate deeply with your spirit, interests, and comfort. Let's lace up our metaphorical boots and walk through the process of picking appealing and incredibly fulfilling destinations for senior travelers like you.

Destinations that Resonate with Senior Travelers

Picking a destination is much like choosing a new book. You want something that piques your interest, matches your mood, and is accessible enough to enjoy without a magnifying glass or a translator! Let's talk about how your interests can guide your choice. If you're a history buff, the ancient ruins of Athens might call to you. If you lean toward culinary adventures, the spice markets of Marrakech will tantalize your senses. Art lovers might find their paradise wandering through the Louvre or along the vibrant streets of Barcelona, rich with Gaudí's whimsical architecture.

Every seasoned traveler, particularly seniors, values comfort and ease. Thus, understanding what makes a destination 'senior-friendly' is key. Accessibility is paramount—look for places known for their well-organized public transport, minimal walking distances, and readily available amenities. Healthcare facilities are another crucial factor. Destinations with reputable healthcare, readily available pharmacies, and easy clinic access offer priceless peace of mind. Safety standards and the availability of senior discounts can also sway your decision. After all, who doesn't appreciate a thoughtful discount at museums, parks, or on public transport?

Seasonal considerations also play a significant role in the planning process. Weather conditions can affect everything from your pack to how much you enjoy wandering around. For instance, avoid the Caribbean during hurricane season or the Middle East during the peak of summer heat. Also, consider the local events happening at the time of your visit. Festivals can be wonderfully enriching, but they can also mean crowded streets and booked-up hotels. Research can help you find the best time to visit, balancing good weather with thinner crowds.

Speaking of research, let's arm you with the best tools for the job. The World Wide Web is your oyster when it comes to travel resources. Start with travel blogs that offer personal insights and up-to-date information. Sites like Nomadic Matt or Senior

Nomads feature tips and stories from fellow travelers that might inspire your next destination. Traditional guidebooks like Lonely Planet or Rick Steves provide comprehensive details on various destinations and are particularly useful for practical information. Online forums such as TripAdvisor or the Thorn Tree forums by Lonely Planet are invaluable for getting first-hand advice from other travelers. And let's not forget the importance of staying informed about travel advisories and health guidelines, especially in today's world; government websites like travel.state.gov or the CDC provide crucial information that could be vital for safe travel planning.

Interactive Element: Destination Decision Chart

Here's a simple exercise to help you visualize your perfect travel destination based on personal interests and practical considerations. Create a chart with columns labeled 'Interests,' 'Accessibility,' 'Healthcare,' 'Safety,' and 'Seasonal Considerations.' Under each, jot down what's most important to you. For instance, under 'Interests,' you might write 'art and culture,' and under 'Accessibility,' you might prioritize 'good public transport.' This visual can help you narrow down destinations that will not only intrigue but also accommodate you beautifully.

Choosing the right travel destination is much like picking the perfect hat for a sunny day—it should be functional and stylish, protective yet comfortable. As you ponder over maps and brochures, remember that the best choice will resonate with both your heart and your practical needs, ensuring that your travels are as enjoyable as they are memorable. Now, with your destinations in mind and a heart full of anticipation, let's look forward to the adventures that await. The world is vast, and its wonders are within your reach—each place has its own story, inviting you to write your chapter. Happy planning!

Budgeting for Your Dream Vacation

Ah, budgeting—the less glamorous side of travel planning, but just as crucial as picking your perfect getaway spot. Think of it as the blueprint that ensures your castle in the sky (or beachside villa) doesn't crumble under financial surprises. Getting your finances in order isn't just about counting pennies; it's about making smart choices that maximize your enjoyment and minimize stress. Let's walk through crafting a travel budget that respects your wallet while splashing a little extravagance on those dream experiences.

First things first, outline all expected expenses. Transportation can be a hefty chunk of your budget, so consider all aspects—flights, trains, rental cars, and even scenic ferry rides. Next up, accommodations. Prices vary wildly, whether you favor hotels, bed and breakfasts, or vacation rentals, so this needs careful consideration. Don't forget the daily essentials like food—will you be dining out for every meal, or does your accommodation allow for the occasional home-cooked dish? Activities, from museum entries to guided tours, also need a line in your budget, and it's wise to set aside a little extra for those spontaneous adventures—the once-in-a-lifetime kind that just can't be passed up. Lastly, always, always have a buffer for emergencies. Whether it's a lost passport or a need for a sudden hotel change, having a financial cushion can turn a potential disaster into a mere hiccup.

Now, let's talk about saving strategies. Booking in advance is often touted as the golden rule for thriftier travel, and for good reason. Airlines, trains, and hotels can offer significant discounts for early birds. Traveling off-season is another wallet-friendly tip, and it comes with the bonus of avoiding the tourist crowds. You might miss the peak weather, but the trade-off can be worth it with cheaper prices and more authentic local interactions.

Regarding accommodations, consider alternatives like Airbnb or even home exchanges, which can offer more bang for your buck than traditional hotels. For dining, why not mix in some meals at local food markets or eateries recommended by locals? They're often cheaper and tastier than the tourist traps.

Scouring deals and discounts specifically for seniors can also stretch your budget. Many airlines offer senior discounts, so don't hesitate to ask when booking. The same goes for accommodations and attractions. Places like museums, parks, and even some restaurants might have price reductions for seniors. Always carry your ID or any membership card that could net you those savings. And remember, your status as a senior traveler comes with wisdom and perks—embrace them!

Lastly, let's talk tech. Financial tools and apps can be lifesavers when managing your travel budget. Apps like Mint or PocketGuard help you keep track of expenses in real time, ensuring you stay on budget without the need for old-school spreadsheets. They can categorize your spending, alert you when you're nearing your limits, and even offer savings tips. For currency conversion, XE Currency is a handy tool that provides live exchange rates, helping you make smarter spending decisions on the go. For those who like to keep things meticulously organized, TripIt keeps your itinerary in order and tracks your expenses related to those plans.

Crafting a detailed travel budget might sound like a chore, but it's about paving the road to a stress-free vacation. With each dollar allocated wisely, you free yourself to fully immerse in the joys of travel—savoring that extra scoop of gelato, saying yes to the impromptu river cruise, or picking up that quirky souvenir that just screams 'you.' So, plan well, spend smarter, and let every cent contribute to making truly priceless memories. After all, isn't that what traveling in this splendid chapter of life is all about?

Travel Insurance: Navigating Your Needs and Options

When it comes to travel, especially for those of us with a bit of gray hair, being prepared is just as important as having your passport. While we all hope for vacations filled with smooth sailings and postcard-worthy sunsets, the unexpected can—and does—happen. That's where travel insurance steps in, not just as a safety net but as an essential travel buddy. Think of travel insurance as that sensible friend who reminds you to bring an umbrella when there's a slight chance of rain. But it's more than just weather; it covers everything from lost luggage to, more critically, health emergencies.

Understanding the ins and outs of travel insurance is key. Typically, a good policy covers trip cancellations, interruptions, medical emergencies, and even evacuations. Why is it crucial, particularly for seniors? As we age, the likelihood of needing medical attention increases, and being in a foreign country can complicate things. Imagine needing a doctor's visit in Paris or, heaven forbid, more intensive care in a place far from home. International healthcare can be astronomically expensive, and Medicare often doesn't cover expenses outside the U.S. Travel insurance can shield you from these potential financial pitfalls, ensuring that a bout of bad health doesn't turn into a financial crisis.

Choosing the right policy is like finding the perfect shoe; it must suit the terrain well. Consider factors like age, pre-existing conditions, the nature of your trip, and its duration. Policies vary, and what works for a weekend getaway might not suffice for a three-month cruise. If you have a pre-existing condition, look for plans that offer a waiver for such conditions; without this, you might find your claims denied under the guise of a pre-existing clause. The length and nature of your trip are also crucial in your decision. Are you going on a relaxing beach vacation or planning to skydive in New Zealand? Higher-risk activities require more comprehensive coverage.

Reading the fine print on your travel insurance policy isn't just good practice—it's essential. Understanding what's covered and, just as importantly, what can save you from surprises when you least need them. Pay attention to the details of medical coverage—does it include just the basics, or does it extend to emergency evacuation and hospital stays? What about the logistics of making a claim? Some policies require upfront payment for services rendered abroad, which you later reclaim. Knowing this can help you prepare financially and mentally. Also, check the protocol for cancellations; some policies offer 'Cancel for Any Reason' coverage, which, while more expensive, provides broader protection.

To get you started on the right foot, here are a few travel insurance providers known for their robust coverage and excellent service, especially favorable to senior travelers: TravelEx, Allianz Global Assistance, and InsureMyTrip. These providers offer a range of plans that cater to different needs and budgets, and they have reputations for straightforward claim processes—a crucial factor when you're in a pinch.

Navigating the world of travel insurance is like trekking through a dense forest. Still, with the right information and guidance, you can find a policy that provides peace of mind, letting you focus on the joys of travel rather than the what-ifs. Armed with your perfect travel insurance plan, you're more ready than ever to embrace the adventures waiting just around the corner. With your safety net firmly in place, you can boldly step into your travels, knowing you're well-prepared for whatever comes your way.

As we wrap up this chapter on navigating your needs and options for travel insurance, remember the key points: understanding what typical policies include, choosing the right plan based on personal health and trip details, diligently reading the policy fine print, and selecting a reputable provider. Equipped with this knowledge, you're not just planning a trip but ensuring a smoother, more secure adventure. Now, with your travel insurance tucked neatly alongside your other plans, we focus on the exciting world of solo and group dynamics in travel. Whether you're thinking of flying solo or joining a group, the next chapter will explore how to make the most of both experiences, ensuring your travel is as enriching as enjoyable.

FOUR

Solo and Group Dynamics

Picture this: you're stepping off the plane in a bustling foreign city, your heart fluttering like a high schooler on the first day of class. But here's the twist—you're flying solo, armed with nothing but your wits, a well-packed suitcase, and a thirst for adventure. Solo travel, especially in the golden years, is like fine wine—rich, refreshing, and wonderfully freeing. It's your show; you're the director and the star. Every decision is yours, from which landmark to visit to where to dine. This chapter dives into the solo travel scene, guiding you through the empowering journey of self-discovery and independence that awaits.

The Liberating Experience of Solo Travel

Empowerment through Independence

Traveling alone isn't just about geographical mobility—it's about moving through personal boundaries and discovering inner strengths you never knew you had. Imagine navigating the metro in Paris, ordering tapas in Spanish at a bustling bar in Madrid, or haggling in a Turkish bazaar—all on your own. Each small victory not only boosts your confidence but also stitches a richer narrative into the fabric of your life, proving that age is no barrier to adventurous living.

The beauty of solo travel lies in its absolute freedom. You can start your day at dawn to catch the first light hitting the ancient stones of Angkor Wat or linger over coffee while people-watching in a Venetian café. This travel molds perfectly around your preferences, pace, and pleasures. And with this freedom comes a profound sense of accomplishment. You're not just accumulating stamps in your passport; you're collecting experiences that say, "I did this on my own!" This is about living your travel dreams on your terms, and there's a tremendous power in that realization, one that resonates deeply long after the suitcase is unpacked.

Building a Solo Travel Plan

Crafting a solo travel itinerary is like painting on a blank canvas—you get to decide what comes next. Start with your interests. Are you an art lover, a history buff, or a culinary enthusiast? Let these passions guide your destination choices. Next, consider your comfort and safety. Research destinations are known for being friendly and safe for solo travelers and are considered easy to travel and communicate with.

When planning, detail is your friend. Map out how you'll get from point A to point B, know the opening hours of attractions, and, most importantly, always have a plan for staying connected. A good tip is to carry a small, portable Wi-Fi device or ensure your mobile plan covers the areas you're visiting. Apps like Google Maps and Citymapper can be lifesavers when navigating unfamiliar cities. Also, always let someone at home know your itinerary—safety is paramount, and this ensures someone always has your back.

Connecting with Locals and Other Travelers

One of the richest aspects of traveling solo is meeting new people, each with unique stories and insights. Engaging with locals and fellow travelers can transform your journey from a mere visit to a vibrant exchange of cultures and ideas. But how do you break the ice? Start simple. A smile, a greeting, or a question can open doors. Joining local tours enriches your understanding of the place and connects you with others who share your curiosity.

Technology also offers a fantastic bridge to new friendships. Apps like Meetup or Facebook groups can connect you with events or gatherings that align with your interests. Whether it's a walking tour, a cooking class, or a local music night, these are opportunities to mingle and share experiences in a natural setting. Remember, every interaction is a chance to learn and grow, adding layers to your solo travel experience that are both enriching and exhilarating.

Overcoming Loneliness

While solo travel is liberating, it can also bring moments of loneliness. This is where technology can again play a comforting role. Keeping in touch with family and friends via video calls or social media can make the world feel smaller and your support network stronger. But don't stop there—immerse yourself in local activities. Attend a workshop, a lecture, or a community event. Such engagements are distracting and deeply enriching, allowing you to feel a part of something larger.

Another delightful way to combat loneliness is to keep a travel journal. Documenting your journey isn't just a way to preserve memories; it's a method of processing experiences and reflecting on the personal growth that travel invariably brings. This can transform solitary moments into opportunities for self-reflection and creativity, turning what might feel like isolation into valuable solitude.

Traveling solo as a senior isn't just about visiting new places; it's about personal growth and discovery. It challenges you, broadens your perspective, and adds to the richness of your life. When you travel alone, you embrace new opportunities for growth and freedom. So, pack your bag, grab your passport, and get ready to explore the world and learn more about yourself. The journey is yours to take, and the possibilities are endless.

Group Travel: Finding Your Tribe and Traveling Together

When you think about traveling in a group, imagine this: a mix of stories, shared laughter over dinners in distant places, and the comforting presence of companions who are just as excited to explore the world as you are. Group travel for seniors isn't just about being part of a crowd; it's about finding your tribe—people who share similar interests and a similar pace, making every step of the adventure enjoyable and accessible.

Choosing the right group tour is like picking the right book club—you need to find one that matches your pace and interests. For travel, this means considering tours that cater specifically to senior travelers. These are not just about slower paces but also thoughtful itineraries that are mindful of energy levels and frequent breaks. Look for tours that balance sightseeing with ample downtime, offer comfortable accommodations, and perhaps most importantly, provide medical support or quick access to healthcare facilities. The size of the group also matters. Smaller groups offer a more personalized experience, which can be less overwhelming and offer more chances to forge deeper connections with fellow travelers.

The benefits of meandering through new cities or ancient ruins with peers are manifold. There's a shared joy in experiencing new cultures and landscapes with others with similar life experiences and perspectives. This camaraderie often turns into lasting friendships, extending well beyond the trip. Traveling in a group also alleviates the stress of planning and logistics. Itineraries are pre-arranged, transportation is taken care of, and activities are set up—all you need to do is show up and immerse yourself in the experience. Moreover, there's an inherent safety in numbers. Whether navigating through a crowded market or dealing with an unexpected detour, having guides and a group around you can make the unfamiliar much less daunting.

However, group dynamics can sometimes be challenging. Differing interests and energy levels can create friction, but these hurdles are manageable. Clear communication from the get-go can help manage expectations. Most tour companies offer itineraries beforehand, so review these and discuss any concerns or needs with your tour guide early on. If you're an early riser who treasures quiet morning walks, you could organize a small group within the group to join you. Flexibility and patience are key—remember, the beauty of group travel lies in the variety of experiences and personalities each member brings to the table.

Customizing your group travel experience can also significantly enhance your satisfaction. Most tour operators are willing to accommodate special requests if made in advance. If you are interested in local cuisine, ask if a cooking class with a local chef can be incorporated into the itinerary. Or, if a particular museum or historical site on the route has always been on your bucket list, check if there's room in the schedule for a visit. Don't hesitate to express your interests—this is your adventure, too.

Traveling with others offers a unique blend of support, social interaction, and shared joy. It provides a structured yet enriching way to explore the world, leaving you with not just photos and souvenirs but new friendships and unforgettable stories. As you venture out with your chosen group, each destination becomes a backdrop to the laughter, shared stories, and discoveries you'll treasure long after returning home.

Combining Solo and Group Travel

Imagine crafting a travel experience that marries the autonomy of solo adventures with the camaraderie and ease of group tours. Sounds like having your cake and eating it, too. It's possible and can lead to a uniquely fulfilling way to explore the world. This hybrid approach allows you to relish the company of like-minded travelers for part of your journey, then spread your wings and fly solo for another segment. Let's delve into how you can strategically blend these travel styles to create a rich, layered experience that satisfies your desire for independence and your appreciation for structured exploration.

Strategic Planning for Mixed Travel

The key to a successful mixed travel experience lies in thoughtful planning. Begin by identifying your main destination or destinations. Consider starting with a group tour in a region that's either logistically complex or culturally challenging. For example, a group tour in India can help you acclimate to the bustling environment with the support of a guide and a ready-made itinerary. After you've gained confidence and a sense of the lay of the land, you might transition into a solo segment in a nearby area like Sri Lanka or Nepal, where you can venture a bit more independently but still benefit from the regional familiarity you've built up.

When planning this type of trip, flexibility is your best friend. Look for group tours that offer built-in free days or optional activities. This setup provides structured experiences with the group while allowing personal time to explore on your terms. Travel companies that cater to senior travelers often design their itineraries with balance in mind, understanding that different travelers have varying appetites for adventure and relaxation. Don't hesitate to discuss your intentions with the tour operator —they can often provide insights or even tailor aspects of the tour to align with your plans for solo travel extensions.

Flexibility and Freedom

Flexibility in travel isn't just about choosing between rest and exploration; it's about allowing space for spontaneous experiences and personal growth. When part of a tour, take advantage of the structured outings to places that might be harder to access, like remote archaeological sites or restricted natural reserves. Then, use your solo time to linger in places that capture your heart or pursue interests the group might not cater to, like a cooking class, a photography walk, or a local music event.

This approach enriches your travel experience and empowers you to follow your curiosity at a pace that suits you without feeling tethered to a group schedule. It's about creating pockets of personal time within a framework of security and company, which can be particularly comforting in unfamiliar territories.

Safety in Numbers

Starting your trip within a group setting offers numerous advantages, especially regarding safety. Navigating the initial challenges of a new country—like understanding local customs, currency, and transportation options—is often easier with a knowledgeable leader's guidance and fellow travelers' support. This is particularly reassuring in regions where language barriers might pose significant challenges or cultural nuances can impact daily interactions.

Once you've gained insight and confidence from your group experience, transitioning to solo travel feels less daunting. You're more familiar with the cultural terrain and better equipped to handle surprises when exploring alone. Additionally, the friendships and connections you've made during the group phase can provide a safety net; there's comfort in knowing there are people who know your whereabouts and can be reached if needed.

Sharing Experiences

The beauty of mixing solo and group travel is that it gives you a range of experiences to share, not just with the new friends you make but also with your broader circle back home. Documenting these varied experiences through a blog, a photo journal, or even a series of emails can enrich your reflections, allowing you to see how different settings and dynamics influence your travel experience. Sharing allows you to connect with others over your adventures and is a valuable resource for those contemplating similar journeys.

This mix of solo and group travel lets you explore the world flexibly and comfortably. You get the freedom of traveling alone with the convenience of group tours. You'll have a meaningful and personal journey by planning well, staying flexible, enjoying the safety of being in a group, and sharing your experiences.

As we wrap up this exploration of solo and group dynamics in travel, remember the key elements that make mixed travel so rewarding: strategic planning, flexibility, safety, and sharing. Each component plays a crucial role in crafting a journey that's as secure as it is liberating. Next, we venture into the world of health and safety on the road, ensuring you're equipped with the knowledge to keep your travels as smooth and enjoyable as possible. Happy travels await, with the freedom to explore and the wisdom to navigate your adventures smartly and safely.

FIVE

Health and Safety First

Let's be honest: the most thrilling part of a rollercoaster is knowing that you're strapped in safely and soundly, ready to enjoy the ups and downs without a care in the world. Just like that, maintaining your health and safety while traveling allows you to fully embrace the joys and surprises of your journey without unnecessary worries niggling at the back of your mind. This chapter is about packing that invisible first aid kit—regarding the right preparations, habits, and know-how—that will keep you cruising smoothly through your adventures, no matter where you are.

Staying Healthy on the Road

Pre-Travel Health Check

Before zipping up that suitcase, let's discuss the all-important health check-up. Visiting your doctor or a travel health clinic before you travel is like having a mini safety briefing before a flight. It's your chance to make sure everything's in working order and to get the green light from a professional. This is about more than just getting the necessary vaccinations. However, those are crucial depending on your destination—no one wants their exotic getaway upstaged by something preventable like yellow fever or Hepatitis A.

Your pre-travel check-up is also the perfect opportunity to review your prescriptions and ensure you have enough to cover the trip, plus a little extra in case of delays. Discuss your existing medical conditions and how they might be affected by travel, from heart issues that could be impacted by high altitudes to arthritis that might flare up in colder climates. And don't forget to talk about travel health insurance because, let's face it, peace of mind is the one travel companion you shouldn't leave home without.

Fitness for Travel

Staying active might not sound as glamorous as sipping margaritas by the beach, but it has perks. Keeping fit can significantly enhance your travel experience by giving you the stamina to explore those cobblestone streets or ancient ruins that much longer. Start with simple routines a few weeks before your departure. Gentle exercises like walking, swimming, or yoga can boost your endurance and improve your flexibility, which is handy when squeezing into a tour bus seat.

While on your trip, integrate physical activity into your itinerary in fun and enjoyable ways. Opt for a walking tour instead of a bus tour, take the stairs in museums or cathedrals instead of the elevator, and if you're feeling adventurous, why not try a dance class? Salsa in Cuba, anyone? Keeping active doesn't just maintain your fitness; it enhances your connection with the places you're exploring, making for richer, more memorable experiences.

Eating Well While Traveling

Navigating new cuisines is one of the tastiest aspects of travel, but it comes with challenges, especially when you have dietary restrictions or health concerns. Start by doing a little homework on the local cuisine—what are the staple foods, common cooking methods, and traditional dishes? This can help you identify options you can enjoy without worry. Don't hesitate to communicate your dietary needs at restaurants—most places are more than willing to accommodate requests, whether it's low-sodium, gluten-free, or vegetarian adjustments.

A good tip is to balance indulgence with moderation. Try that rich, delicious pastry or deep-fried street food only for a few days. Complement these treats with fresh fruits, vegetables, and plenty of fluids, especially water, to keep you hydrated and feeling your best. Healthy snacks like almonds, oat bars, or dried fruit can save the day when healthy options are scarce during long excursions or in remote areas.

Mental Health and Wellness

Traveling can be a profound source of joy, but let's not brush aside the stress it can sometimes bring. Long flights, time zone changes, and a packed itinerary can take their toll. Managing your mental well-being is as important as keeping physically healthy. Try to incorporate routines from home into your travel schedule, like morning meditation or a bedtime reading ritual, to give your days structure and familiarity.

Jet lag can be a real party pooper, so ease its impact by adjusting your schedule gradually a few days before your trip. Once at your destination, try to sync with the local time as soon as possible—yes, that might mean pushing through a sleepy afternoon with a gentle walk instead of a nap. Keeping your stress levels low also means not overpacking your itinerary. Leave room for downtime, whether it's a leisurely afternoon in a café or a rest day between heavy tour days. Remember, this is your time to recharge, not run a marathon.

Traveling is your time to shine, explore, and experience the world in all its glory. By keeping your body tuned and your mind sharp, you're not just preparing for a trip but setting the stage for an adventure that's as healthy as happy. So, take care of yourself, and the world will take care of you, offering its wonders one incredible moment at a time.

Safety Tips: Avoiding Common Pitfalls

Traveling the world as a senior is exciting, with many new things to see and hear. However, it also means being aware and prepared to avoid potential issues. Let's start with the basics—keeping your valuables secure. It's easy to get caught up in the excitement of a bustling marketplace or the beauty of a scenic overlook, but this is also when you should heighten your vigilance. A cross-body bag with a secure closure is more secure than a shoulder bag or a backpack, which can be more easily snatched or stealthily unzipped. Consider using bags with RFID-blocking technology to protect your credit cards and passports from electronic pickpocketing—a modern thief doesn't need to grab your wallet to steal from you!

Moreover, staying alert can be balanced while exploring these exciting environments. Crowded places are prime spots for petty thieves. Keep a watchful eye on your belongings and be wary of distractions—thieves often work in teams where one will divert your attention while another makes off with your goods. Also, a simple rule when mingling in crowded areas is to keep your bag in front of you and your hand over the opening or lock.

Let's shift gears to getting around safely. Public transportation can be a fantastic way to travel like a local, but it comes with challenges. Before boarding a bus or train, do homework to understand the safest and most reliable options. Many cities have apps for their public transit systems that provide real-time updates and maps. When using taxis, especially in foreign countries, it's prudent to use official taxi services—preferably booked through your hotel or a recognized app. If you rent a vehicle, familiarize yourself with the local road rules beforehand. In many places, you can find driving customs dramatically different from what you're used to at home, and navigating an unknown terrain can be stressful if unprepared.

Another crucial part of travel safety is being prepared for emergencies. Before you set out each day, make sure your phone is fully charged, and you have backup power in the form of a portable charger. Keep a small card in your wallet with essential local emergency numbers, your accommodation address, and a contact number for someone back home who can assist in an emergency. Technology can also be a lifesaver here—apps like TripWhistle Global SOS provide you with local emergency numbers and send your GPS coordinates to emergency services if you're unsure of your location.

Now, onto a less pleasant topic, but one that's crucial to address—travel scams. These can range from overly aggressive street vendors to sophisticated online booking scams. The rule of thumb here is if something feels off, it probably is. Be skeptical of unsolicited help with luggage or navigation, especially if it comes with a request for money. And while the internet is a fantastic tool for booking your travels, ensure you use reputable sites and check reviews when planning your activities or stays. Always compare offers from different sources; scammers often lure unsuspecting tourists with prices significantly lower than the market rate. Remember, a deal that seems too good to be true might be.

Navigating through these safety tips ensures a smoother trip and empowers you to focus on the joys of travel rather than the worries. With your safety strategies packed alongside your essentials, every destination becomes closer to feeling like a home away from home.

Managing Medications and Health Conditions Abroad

Let's chat about a topic that might not be the highlight of your travel plans but is certainly crucial—managing your medications and health conditions while gallivanting around the globe. Imagine you're all set for a sunrise photo shoot at Machu Picchu, but you left your heart medication in your other bag back in Cusco. A bit of pre-planning can ensure that your health stays on track, no matter where your travels take you.

Managing medications while traveling isn't just about packing them; it's about organizing them to keep you in the pink of health throughout your trip. First, keep a detailed list of all your medications, including their generic names—not all countries use the same brand names, and you'll want to avoid confusion. It's also wise to carry a note from your doctor explaining your medications, their necessity, and any medical conditions they treat. This can be a godsend at border controls, especially since some legal and commonly prescribed medications at home might be restricted in other countries. Always check the regulations for medicines in the countries you visit to avoid any unwelcome surprises at customs.

For actual packing, think of accessibility and redundancy. Divide your medication into two batches—keep one with you in your carry-on (never check your medications in case your luggage decides to take a different holiday) and another packed elsewhere. This way, you're covered if one set gets lost. Consider investing in a pill organizer—a simple, foolproof way to keep track of your doses, making it easier to stay on schedule, especially when jet lag or a packed itinerary might throw you off your usual routine.

When accessing healthcare services abroad, a little research goes a long way. Know where the nearest pharmacy and hospital are to where you'll be staying. Many countries have well-stocked pharmacies and often offer medications over the counter that might require a prescription back home. However, the assurance of getting exactly what you need when you need it is comforting. Apps like Google Maps can be helpful to locate these facilities quickly, or even better, ask your hotel or host for recommendations—they usually know the ins and outs of the neighborhood.

Navigating foreign healthcare systems can be daunting, but remember, you're rarely alone. Most embassies and consulates can guide nearby medical services. This brings us to the importance of travel insurance—make sure you opt for a comprehensive medical coverage policy. This should ideally cover everything from doctor visits, and hospital stays to potential medical evacuation because while it's unlikely you'll need to be airlifted out of a remote location if it happens, you'll thank your lucky stars for that coverage. Before you travel, understand exactly how your insurance works—is there a direct billing agreement, or will you need to pay upfront and claim later? This can affect how you budget for your trip.

And let's touch on a scenario we all prefer to avoid—medical emergencies. They can be stressful, especially in a foreign land where the language and procedures might be unfamiliar. Always carry a card in your wallet with your emergency contact, blood type, known allergies, and any chronic conditions listed. You can dial an emergency number in many places for immediate assistance, but knowing a few basic phrases in the local language can help, too. Phrases like "I need a doctor" or "Please help" can bridge the gap while you wait for assistance. Additionally, keep a digital copy of your medical records accessible in your email or cloud storage—for medical staff, understanding your history is crucial in emergencies.

Traveling with health conditions or managing medications shouldn't deter you from seeing the world. With some smart planning, the right precautions, and a bit of savvy, you can enjoy your travels with peace of mind, knowing you're as prepared as can be. So, pack your medications, organize your documents, and prepare for a hassle-free adventure.

As we close this chapter on health and safety, remember that a well-prepared traveler is happy. From managing medications to navigating local healthcare, each step you take toward preparation allows you to embark confidently on your travels. Next, we'll dive into the exciting world of special interest travel, exploring how hobbies and passions can translate into unforgettable travel experiences. Ready to see how your interests can shape your next adventure? Let's go!

SIX

Special Interest and Hobby-Based Travel

Have you ever imagined turning your travel adventures into a delicious expedition where every meal opens up a new page of your culinary diary? Welcome to the world of culinary tours, where your love for food enhances your travel experiences, turning each destination into a feast for the senses. In this chapter, we'll explore how you, as a senior traveler, can deepen your travel experiences by engaging with global cuisines, from the bustling night markets of Taipei to the refined, Michelin-starred eateries of Paris. So, tighten your apron, sharpen your palate, and let's dive into the flavorful world of culinary tourism.

Culinary Tours: A Taste of the World

Exploring Global Cuisines

Imagine strolling through the vibrant streets of Marrakech, where the air is thick with the scent of saffron and cumin, or sitting down to a plate of fresh, zesty ceviche at a seaside shack in Lima. Culinary travel is about more than just eating; it's about connecting with cultures through the universal language of food. Each spoonful of gazpacho or bite of nigiri is a story—a blend of history, tradition, and local flavor. I want to enjoy each culinary experience without feeling rushed, fully savor these stories, appreciate the nuances of each dish, and understand the journey of ingredients from farm to table. Whether indulging in pastries in a Viennese café or exploring the spicy wonders of an Indian street food stall, each culinary experience enriches your travel story, adding flavors that linger long after the trip ends.

Culinary Tour Companies for Seniors

Choosing the right culinary tour can significantly enhance your travel experience, especially when the tour is tailored to fit the pace and preferences of senior travelers. Companies like Road Scholar and ElderTreks offer culinary tours designed with seniors in mind, focusing on accessibility and a leisurely pace that allows you to enjoy each culinary experience without feeling rushed fully. These tours often include visits to local producers—like cheese artisans in Switzerland or vineyards in Tuscany—where you can learn about the production processes and sample the delicious outcomes. The beauty of these tours is that they handle all the logistics, from transportation to food allergies, ensuring you can indulge your culinary curiosities stress-free.

Cooking Classes and Market Visits

There's something truly magical about turning a basket of fresh, local ingredients into a traditional dish under the guidance of a skilled chef. Participating in cooking classes during travels offers a hands-on way to connect with the local cuisine. It's not just about following a recipe; it's about learning the stories behind the dishes, the secret tweaks that make a local dish authentic, and the joy of sharing the meal you helped prepare with fellow food lovers. Similarly, visiting local markets can be a feast for the senses. The colors, the smells, and the sounds of a bustling food market can give you deeper insight into the heart of a culture than any museum or monument. So, roll up your sleeves, pick up that chef's knife, and let the local flavors guide you to delicious discoveries.

Documenting Culinary Adventures

What's a feast without some stories to go with it? Keeping a food diary or starting a culinary blog is a great way to document and share your food adventures. Whether you're writing down recipes, sketching a busy spice market, or snapping a photo of your morning espresso, these records become a collection of tasty memories. Sharing your experiences on Instagram or a personal blog lets you relive your culinary adventures and inspire others to explore the world through food. It's also a great way to connect with other food-loving travelers who can share tips and recommendations. Whether it's the tang of a lemon tart in Amalfi or the rich aroma of Turkish coffee in Istanbul, each note and photo adds to your travel experiences.

For senior travelers, a culinary tour is about enjoying the world with all your senses, turning each meal into a moment of connection, and making each taste a lasting memory. Let your love of food guide you to new places, enrich your travels with flavors, and keep your adventurous spirit alive. Enjoy your meals and happy travels!

Exploring the Great Outdoors: Bird Watching and Nature Hikes

There's nothing quite like the thrill of spotting a rare bird in its natural habitat or a sense of accomplishment after a scenic hike. For those of you who cherish the rustle of leaves underfoot and the chirping of birds overhead, combining bird watching with nature hikes presents a delightful way to engage with the outdoors. Let's talk gear first because comfort and safety are paramount, especially when you're out enjoying the beauty of nature. Whether you're an experienced birder or a casual nature walker, the right equipment can make all the difference. Start with a good pair of binoculars, the birdwatcher's best friend. Opt for a lightweight model with strong magnification to make those distant sightings clearer and more thrilling. A comfortable harness replaces the traditional neck strap to distribute weight evenly across your shoulders, reducing neck strain during those long walks.

Now, sturdy footwear is essential—choose waterproof hiking boots with good ankle support and non-slip soles to handle varied terrains, from muddy paths to rocky inclines. Don't forget a weather-appropriate hat and layered clothing to adapt to changing conditions throughout the day. A lightweight, waterproof backpack is also crucial for carrying your snacks and water but for stowing away those extra layers as the day warms up. Packing a first aid kit, a whistle for emergencies, and a portable GPS or a map can also boost your confidence on the trail, ensuring you're prepared for whatever the day might throw at you.

Finding trails and destinations that cater to your comfort and safety needs doesn't have to be a chore. Many national parks and nature reserves offer well-maintained trails with varying difficulty levels. Look for locations known for their bird diversity, and check if they have accessible trails marked for less strenuous hiking. These paths are often well-paved or boardwalked, making them perfect for those who prefer a more relaxed pace while still enjoying the beautiful scenery and wildlife. Before you set out, check the weather conditions and trail reviews from other senior hikers—many websites and forums offer real-time updates and advice that can help you choose the perfect trail for your day in nature.

Embracing the community aspect of bird watching and hiking can significantly enhance your experience. Joining a nature group or club brings many benefits, including fellow nature enthusiasts' shared knowledge and camaraderie. These groups often organize outings that can take you to new and exciting birding spots, offer workshops on everything from bird calls to flora identification, and provide a supportive community that makes every outing more enjoyable. Whether it's the local chapter of the Audubon Society or an informal hiking club, being part of a group gives you access to a wealth of shared knowledge and experiences, making each trip a learning opportunity and a social one.

Lastly, let's not overlook the immense benefits that spending time in nature has on your physical and mental well-being. Engaging in outdoor activities like bird watching and hiking boosts your physical health by improving your stamina, balance, and flexibility and enhances your mental health. Nature has a unique way of soothing the mind, reducing stress and anxiety through its tranquil settings and gentle sounds. The focused activity of bird watching, where you tune in to the sights and sounds of the environment, can be particularly meditative. It's a chance to disconnect from the hustle and bustle of daily life and reconnect with the natural world, finding peace and relaxation in the rhythms of nature.

Whether setting out to spot a Snowy Egret or conquer a new trail, bird watching and hiking offer a wonderful escape into the wild. Each step and each sighting brings you closer to the heart of nature's wonders. So, grab your binoculars and hiking boots, and prepare for an adventure that's as rewarding to the body and mind as it is delightful to the senses.

Art and Culture Immersion

Imagine wandering into a world where every brush stroke tells a story, every sculpture speaks a silent language, and every performance echoes the heartbeat of a culture. For those of you with a penchant for the arts, integrating visits to museums, galleries, and local performances into your travel plans can transform a simple trip into an enriching cultural journey. Let's paint a picture of how you can immerse yourself fully in the local art scene, creating memories that are as vibrant as the masterpieces you'll encounter.

Museums and galleries are treasure troves that house the legacies of civilizations, artists, and societies. Whether it's marveling at the intricate details of Renaissance paintings in Italy or exploring contemporary art in a funky gallery in New York City, each venue offers a glimpse into the soul of the place. But don't just wander! Many museums offer guided tours tailored for senior travelers, which can provide richer insights and a more accessible pace. And why not attend a special exhibition or a night event if available? These can offer a more intimate experience of the art, often with fewer crowds and a different atmospheric feel. Engage fully with the experience—bring a sketchbook to capture your impressions or jot down the thoughts and feelings the artworks evoke. It's a wonderful way to preserve and reflect on the experience later.

Local performances, on the other hand, add a dynamic layer to your cultural exploration. From traditional dances that tell the tales of ancient myths to modern theatrical productions that challenge contemporary norms, each performance is a window into the community's values, struggles, and joys. Don't shy away from smaller, perhaps less polished, local performances either—these often hold the raw authenticity that more commercial shows may lack. Check local event listings or ask your hotel for recommendations on performances happening around you. Often, attending a local show not only supports the arts within the community but can also be a gateway to interacting with locals afterward, sharing impressions and interpretations.

Participating in art and culture workshops offers a hands-on approach to understanding local traditions and crafts. Imagine learning batik in Indonesia, pottery in Morocco, or calligraphy in China. These workshops allow you to learn a new skill and engage directly with artisans who are bearers of their craft's history and techniques. These interactions can be profoundly moving, as they are as much about the exchange of stories and ideas as they are about the craft itself. Many communities have local arts centers or cultural hubs where these workshops are offered—places where art is not just made but lived and breathed. Participating in these workshops can give you a deeper appreciation of the skill and history behind each piece, making the souvenirs you might bring home all the more meaningful.

Timing your visits to coincide with cultural festivals and events can dramatically enrich your travel experience. Festivals are like the pulse of a culture, vibrant and alive. They offer a mix of music, dance, food, and art, all wrapped up in one exciting experience. Whether the colorful chaos of India's Holi, the solemn tradition of Japan's Tea Ceremonies during festival times, or the lively jazz festivals in New Orleans, each event offers a unique cultural immersion. Plan, as these festivals are often the year's biggest events for local communities. They offer spectacular experiences that are deeply rooted in local heritage.

Engaging with local artists and communities provides insight into their artistic processes and the cultural narratives that shape their work. Visit local art studios, engage in conversations with artists, and, if possible, participate in community art projects. Many artists are eager to share their stories and might even offer more personalized tours of their galleries or studios. These interactions enrich your understanding and create connections that bridge cultures and continents.

Art and culture are more than just things to see; they're about getting involved and connecting. By including these elements in your travels, you enhance your trip and deepen your understanding of the world. Each painting, performance, and craft you experience offers a new perspective, making your travels richer and more meaningful.

As we close this chapter on art and culture immersion, reflect on how these experiences have not only colored your travels but deepened your connection to the places and people you've encountered. Art, in all its forms, opens doors to new experiences and inner reflections, making your journey richer in ways you can't even imagine. As we turn the page, we look ahead to the next adventure, ready to explore, learn, and connect more.

SEVEN

Hidden Gems Across the Globe

Have you ever woken up and thought, "Today, I want to wander somewhere less wandered?" If you're nodding, this chapter is your new travel buddy, ready to whisk you away to the less-trodden paths of Eastern Europe. Picture this: you're leisurely strolling through a quaint town where the bakery shop owner knows every customer by name, or you're sipping coffee in a quiet village square, watching the day unfold at an almost poetic pace. With its deep-rooted history, vibrant cultures, and serene landscapes, Eastern Europe offers a treasure chest of destinations perfect for those who appreciate a slower, more meaningful travel rhythm.

The Quiet Charms of Eastern Europe

Cultural Richness

Eastern Europe is full of fascinating history and vibrant culture. The region's lesser-known cities and towns are bursting with historical significance, offering a serene alternative to the often bustling tourist hubs found elsewhere. Take Lviv, Ukraine, for example, with its cozy coffee houses and cobbled streets echoing with tales from the Austro-Hungarian Empire and beyond. Or consider the serene beauty of Lake Bled in Slovenia, where a church-dotted island sits like a jewel amid emerald waters, whispering tales of pilgrims and promises.

Here, every corner has a story, whether through the Gothic architecture of Romania's Transylvania or the thermal baths of Budapest, steaming with legends of healing and royal escapades. Engaging with these stories enriches your travel experience and connects you deeper to the places you visit. Imagine attending an organ concert in a centuries-old church in Krakow or exploring the ancient fortress of Kotor, Montenegro, where every stone is steeped in history. These experiences are not just about sightseeing; they're about time-traveling.

Accessibility and Comfort

Thinking about comfort and accessibility, especially for us seasoned travelers, is not just practical—it's essential. Destinations like Slovenia's Lake Bled and the medieval towns of Romania are perfect examples of places that cater well to the leisurely traveler. You can enjoy a peaceful boat ride to the island or a leisurely walk around the lake at Lake Bled. Both activities are designed to be easily accessible to everyone.

With its step-back-in-time charm, Romania offers easy access to exploring its historic castles and fortresses with guided tours that consider your pace and comfort. Public transport in these regions is also accommodating, with options like buses and trains offering scenic routes that are as relaxing as they are reliable. And let's remember the plethora of cozy, senior-friendly accommodations, from charming bed and breakfasts in Ljubljana to welcoming guesthouses in the Bulgarian countryside, ensuring your stay is as delightful as your explorations.

Local Experiences

Eastern Europe's local scene is a goldmine for those who treasure genuine connections and immersive experiences. Traditional folk music evenings in a Slovakian tavern or a leisurely afternoon at a local craft market in Estonia offer intimate glimpses into the region's soul. These experiences not only forge a deeper connection with the place but also with its people.

Participate in a pottery workshop in Hungary or spend an evening at a wine harvest festival in Moldova. Such activities provide fun and a real hands-on understanding of local traditions and lifestyles. They're opportunities to learn, engage, and collect unique memories crafted by your hands and heart.

Travel Tips

Navigating Eastern Europe, with its diverse languages and customs, can seem daunting, but with a few practical tips, you'll feel right at home. The best times to visit for mild weather and fewer tourists are late spring and early autumn when the landscape bursts into vibrant colors and the tourist crowds thinner.

Language barriers can be navigated with ease nowadays, thanks to technology. Apps like Google Translate or Duolingo can help you learn basic phrases or translate on the go. Most locals appreciate even the smallest attempt at their language, turning simple interactions into warm exchanges. And while you're packing, remember to include a good travel guidebook and a phrasebook, which can enhance your understanding and appreciation of the places you'll visit.

Cultural Immersion Workshop

Consider joining a cultural immersion workshop to connect with Eastern Europe's rich culture. This could involve anything from a traditional cooking class to a folk dance lesson. It's not just about learning a new skill; it's about experiencing the pulse of the place through its traditions and sharing that joy with others. These workshops often lead to meaningful exchanges with locals, providing insights into their way of life and traditions. They're a fun way to meet fellow travelers who share your curiosity and zest for deeper cultural understanding.

As you explore Eastern Europe's quiet charms, remember that traveling here offers more than just a holiday; it provides a journey through history, culture, and heartwarming hospitality. Every step in this region feels like walking through history; every meal gives you a taste of tradition, and every interaction connects you to the rich culture of Eastern European life. So, take your time, soak in the richness, and let the serene beauty of these places fill your travel diary with stories worth retelling.

Southeast Asia's Untouched Paradises

When you think of Southeast Asia, bustling markets and ancient temples come to mind. But let's turn the dial to a different setting, where tranquility reigns and nature's untouched beauty unfolds before you. Imagine yourself on the serene beaches of Palawan in the Philippines, where the sand is so fine and white it feels like powdered sugar under your toes, and the water a myriad of blues that artists spend lifetimes trying to capture on canvas. Or you're more inclined toward Laos's lush, rolling landscapes, where the countryside stretches like a green carpet, dotted with traditional villages and the occasional elephant sauntering by. These paradises offer a retreat from the hustle and bustle and a chance to connect with nature in some of Earth's most stunning, pristine environments.

The beauty of these destinations isn't just in their postcard-perfect vistas; it's also in the senior-friendly facilities that make traveling here a breeze. In Palawan, resorts and lodgings are plentiful, with options ranging from luxurious villas on the beach to more modest but equally charming bungalows surrounded by nature. These places often offer amenities like on-site dining, wellness centers, and assistance with arranging accessible tours that consider mobility needs and comfort. Over in Laos, the accommodation often integrates traditional architecture with modern comforts, ensuring an authentic and relaxing stay. Many of these facilities provide tailored travel experiences, including transport services that make exploring the surrounding areas easy and enjoyable for those who might not be up for a hike through the jungle but still wish to experience its beauty up close.

For those who love to dive deeper into the culture and lifestyle of the places they visit, Southeast Asia offers a plethora of gentle yet enriching cultural immersion activities. For instance, engaging in a traditional cooking class can be a delightful way to spend a morning. Whether learning to make the perfect Pad Thai in Thailand or mastering the art of Vietnamese Pho, these classes often occur in open, airy kitchens or outdoors, guided by local chefs who treat you more like family than tourists.

Meditation retreats are another soul-soothing option available in this region, particularly in Thailand and Cambodia, where the practice is intertwined with the local way of life. These retreats can vary from a few hours to several days, accommodating everyone from beginners to those who have meditated for years, often held in tranquil settings that promote peace and well-being.

One of the most heartwarming experiences is staying in a village homestay, which is quite popular in rural Vietnam and Cambodia. These stays give you a firsthand look at the daily lives of local families and allow you to contribute directly to the community, turning an ordinary vacation into a meaningful exchange. Activities during these homestays can include fishing, weaving, and even helping to prepare meals, all done at a leisurely pace that allows for plenty of relaxation.

Traveling in tropical climates, however, does come with its own set of guidelines to ensure your health and safety remain top priorities. Hydration is key, as the heat and humidity can be more intense than what many travelers are used to. Always carry a bottle of water with you, and don't hesitate to take frequent breaks in shaded areas to cool down. Protecting yourself from insect-borne diseases is also crucial; wearing insect repellent and clothing that covers arms and legs can be effective ways to prevent bites. Most accommodations provide mosquito nets or screens, but it's always good to be prepared with your measures, especially outdoors.

Sun protection is another non-negotiable aspect of traveling in Southeast Asia. The sun here can be particularly strong, so a high SPF sunscreen, a wide-brimmed hat, and UV-protective sunglasses are must-haves in your day pack. Remember, the goal is to enjoy the sun, not to let it sideline you with a burn or heat exhaustion. Taking these precautions allows you to embrace the natural beauty and cultural richness of Southeast Asia's untouched paradises safely and comfortably, making for a travel experience that soothes the soul and ignites the spirit.

Exploring the Natural Beauty of South America

Imagine waking up to the majestic sight of the Andes stretching skyward, their peaks like sentinels guarding South America's rich, textured landscapes. This continent has various landscapes, each with its unique beauty and charm. For seasoned explorers, the geographic diversity from the arid Atacama Desert to the lush Amazon rainforest opens up a playground where adventure and relaxation intersect. Picture yourself sipping a glass of Malbec in the sun-drenched vineyards of Mendoza or perhaps gently cruising the blue waters of Lake Titicaca. South America's varied landscapes are stunning; they beckon for leisurely exploration that suits our pace perfectly.

Now, let's talk about eco-tourism, a style of travel that's fulfilling and deeply respectful of the environments we visit. The Amazon Basin, sprawling across multiple countries, offers an eco-tourism experience. Imagine gliding in a canoe through the verdant rainforest, home to the symphony of parrots and the stealthy jaguar. Eco-lodges tucked away in these rainforests provide the perfect base for wildlife watching, combining comfort with minimal environmental impact. Down south, Patagonia's rugged, wind-swept landscapes host sustainable lodges where the spirit of conservation is as palpable as the breathtaking views. These eco-friendly options allow you to embrace the natural world in ways that foster conservation and local community benefits, aligning your travel with values that support sustainability and preservation.

From ancient civilizations to colonial times, cultural heritage sites across South America offer a window into the continent's layered history. Accessibility to these treasures is increasingly a focus, making them more enjoyable for travelers who appreciate more time and comfort in their explorations. Take, for instance, the ruins of Machu Picchu in Peru. Recent improvements in access mean you can explore this ancient Incan city with greater ease, whether by train or via a more leisurely trek. In Ecuador, the historical center of Quito invites strolls through colonial streets, where accessibility improvements have made exploring its rich history and vibrant local life smoother for those who prefer to take it slow.

Navigating South America is an adventure, with options catering to various comfort levels and travel styles. The continent's extensive network of flights makes jumping from one country to another a relatively swift affair. However, for those who enjoy soaking in the scenery, bus travel in countries like Chile and Argentina offers comfortable and economical options, with premium services featuring reclining seats and onboard meals. For a scenic and serene journey, consider rail journeys like the famous Belmond Andean Explorer in Peru, which combines luxury with breathtaking views through the heart of the Andes.

Exploring South America is like unwrapping a vibrant package, each layer revealing landscapes and cultures more enchanting and engaging. Whether you find yourself wandering through the cobblestone streets of Cartagena, soaking up the Caribbean charm or breathing in the crisp air of Patagonian wilderness, the continent offers a stunning backdrop to a travel experience that's as engaging physically as it is enriching spiritually. Here, the past and present come together in vibrant cultures, stunning landscapes, and warm hospitality, making every moment special. As you plan your South American adventure, remember that this continent invites exploration and rewards the curious and the cautious with experiences as deep and varied as the landscapes themselves. So pack your bags, bring your sense of wonder, and let South America show you its spectacular secrets.

Wrapping Up the Chapter

In our journey through the hidden gems of the globe, we've wandered through the serene charms of Eastern Europe, delved into the untouched paradises of Southeast Asia, and explored the stunning diversity of South America. Each destination offers unique opportunities for sightseeing and deep, enriching experiences that resonate with our seasoned sensibilities. From cultural richness and eco-tourism to accessible travel logistics, these regions beckon with open arms, promising comfortable and captivating adventures. As we close this chapter and look to the next, let's carry forward the spirit of discovery and anticipation, ready to uncover more world secrets. Onward to our next adventure, where new experiences and old friends await.

EIGHT

American Treasures

I magine America as a grand old scrapbook, its pages filled with the majestic landscapes of National Parks, each a testament to nature's artistry. Now, picture yourself leisurely flipping through these pages, where every turn reveals a snapshot of awe-inspiring beauty and tranquility. This isn't just sightseeing; it's about embarking on a serene journey through America's backyard, with each National Park offering a unique story told through ancient rock formations, whispering canyons, and towering forests. This journey is even more delightful because it's tailored for you, ensuring comfort, accessibility, and a treasure trove of memories. Let's explore how you can experience the National Parks through a lens that appreciates travel's finer, slower details, making every moment count without the rush.

National Parks Through a Senior's Lens

Scenic Routes

For those who adore nature but prefer to admire it from a little less distance, the scenic routes and drives within our National Parks are nothing short of spectacular. Imagine cruising along the Going-to-the-Sun Road in Glacier National Park, where each curve offers a new panoramic view of mountain vistas and pristine lakes, all from the comfort of your vehicle. Or, consider the scenic drives through the Smoky Mountains, where the mist-enshrouded peaks create a mystical tableau that unfolds gracefully before your eyes. These drives are not just roads; they are ribbons winding through the heart of America's natural splendor, designed for those who find deep joy in viewing landscapes from their sun-warmed car seats, camera in hand, no hiking boots necessary.

Visitor Programs

The beauty of these parks is matched by their inclusivity, offering a plethora of visitor programs that cater specifically to seniors. Many parks offer guided tours in shuttle buses or trams, where you can soak in the educational richness without worrying about the trail dust. These programs often include talks by rangers who bring the park's history and ecology to life, making each visit not just a tour but a lesson in the grandeur of nature. For those interested in more than just sightseeing, many parks also offer workshops and classes, from photography to bird watching, for leisure and deep learning.

Accommodation Choices

After a day of absorbing the sheer beauty of these parks, knowing you have a cozy place to rest your head makes the experience even sweeter. The accommodation options within and near the parks range from rustic lodges that echo the natural charm around them to comfortable hotels that bring a touch of modernity to the wilderness. Many of these accommodations offer senior-friendly amenities, such as accessible rooms and shuttle services. Whether you stay within the park boundaries or in a nearby town, the blend of comfort and convenience is designed to make your stay as enjoyable as your explorations.

Park Accessibility

Ensuring everyone can access them is vital to today's National Parks experience. Paved paths leading to breathtaking viewpoints, wheelchair-friendly visitor centers, and clear, well-placed signage ensure these natural wonders are open to all, regardless of mobility levels. Parks like Yosemite have led the way with extensive accessibility modifications, ensuring that attractions like the famous Yosemite Falls are just a pleasant stroll away. Information is also readily available through park websites and visitor centers, making it easy to plan your visit around your specific needs and interests, ensuring that the beauty of the wild is always within reach.

Interactive Element: Reflection Section

As you plan your visit to these National Parks, take a moment to reflect on what aspects of nature you love the most. Is it the serene lakes, the majestic mountains, or the wide-open spaces that resonate with you? Jotting down these thoughts can help tailor your trip to your passions, ensuring that each park visit aligns perfectly with your love of nature. This kind of planning makes the trip not just a journey through parks but a personal exploration of your connections to the natural world.

Exploring America's National Parks at a pace that respects both your energy and your curiosity opens up a world of beauty and tranquility, readily accessible and eagerly awaiting your visit. With each park offering its unique landscape and story, your travels through these natural treasures promise to be as enriching as they are breathtaking. So, take the scenic route, engage with the natural history, rest comfortably, and enjoy the accessibility that makes these adventures a joy at any age.

Coastal Retreats for Relaxation

When the world gets a bit too loud, there's nothing quite like the soothing symphony of ocean waves, the soft caress of sea breezes, and the tranquil vistas of the coast to set things right. For those of us who have waved goodbye to the daily grind and are in search of some well-deserved peace, coastal retreats offer a sanctuary where the rhythms of the ocean dictate the pace of the day. Picture yourself on a sun-dappled beach where the only footprints are likely your own or lounging under a palm tree as the afternoon ebbs into a vibrant sunset. These beaches aren't just stretches of sand; they're stretches of serenity tailored for relaxation and rejuvenation.

Take, for instance, the serene shores of Cannon Beach in Oregon, where the iconic Haystack Rock stands guard over a coastline that invites strolls and reflective pauses. Or the gentle beaches of Cape May in New Jersey, where Victorian charm meets ocean tranquility, setting the stage for a calming retreat from the hustle and bustle of city life. These destinations are chosen for their scenic beauty, calm waters, and uncrowded sands, making them perfect for a morning of soulful solitude or an afternoon nap by the sea. The accessibility of these beaches is a thoughtful bonus, with flat, firm pathways and boardwalks that make the beach experience inclusive for everyone, regardless of mobility concerns.

Transitioning from the natural embrace of peaceful beaches, let's consider the nurturing environments of coastal wellness resorts and sanctuaries of health and relaxation. These resorts understand that well-being goes beyond physical health, encompassing a holistic approach to rejuvenating mind, body, and spirit. Imagine a resort on the cliffs of Big Sur, California, where spa treatments are infused with local herbs and the yoga sessions offer panoramic views of the Pacific. Or perhaps a hideaway in the Florida Keys, where nutritional workshops and guided meditation sessions help you recalibrate your lifestyle, surrounded by water on all sides.

These wellness resorts often offer programs specifically designed with seniors in mind—think gentle yoga classes, therapeutic spa treatments, and nutrition plans crafted to enhance vitality and wellness. The slow-paced, attentive approach ensures that each guest can find their rhythm and healing, making these resorts not just places to stay but to renew.

Looking at the cultural life of coastal towns, these charming places offer a mix of relaxation and enrichment, where the sea meets art, history, and great food. As America's oldest city, St. Augustine, Florida, offers cobblestone streets, historic forts, and quaint cafes, all within an accessible, walk-friendly layout that invites exploration without exertion. Similarly, the coastal town of Carmel-by-the-Sea in California, with its fairy-tale cottages and art galleries, makes for a delightful exploration of local art and culture, all set against the backdrop of stunning ocean views.

These towns are not just stops along the coast; they are vibrant communities where seniors can enjoy the local cuisine, delve into the area's history, and experience the arts leisurely. Many coastal towns are known for their senior-friendly atmospheres, offering everything from guided historical tours on smooth, easy paths to local theater productions that captivate and entertain.

Lastly, as we bask in the coastal ambiance, we must have some safety tips to ensure every beach visit is as pleasant as it is memorable. Always wear a broad-spectrum sunscreen to protect yourself from the sun's rays, and stay hydrated, especially when spending extended periods outdoors. Opt for beaches with lifeguard services and gentle terrains to ensure safe swimming and easy walking. Remember, the coast is there for your enjoyment and rejuvenation, so taking these small precautions helps keep your time by the sea as carefree as the ocean breeze.

As you ponder your next retreat, consider the soothing lull of coastal towns, the nurturing embrace of wellness resorts, and the tranquil beauty of serene beaches. Each offers a unique way to unwind, recharge, and enjoy the later chapters of life with the soothing soundtrack of the ocean in the background.

Cultural Deep Dives in America's Historic Cities

Imagine strolling through the cobblestone streets of Boston, where every brick seems steeped in Revolutionary War history or soaking in the soulful sounds of a jazz band in a quaint club in New Orleans. These experiences aren't just walks or concerts; they are lively parts of the rich cultural fabric of America's historic cities. For those who cherish the past and delight in stories told through architecture, festivals, and food, these cities offer a cultural deep dive that feels like a time travel experience tailored just for us.

America's historic cities are treasure troves of heritage and history, offering more than just a glimpse into the past—they invite you to step right in. Take Charleston, for instance, with its beautifully preserved antebellum architecture and horse-drawn carriages that seem to transport you to a bygone era. Or Philadelphia, where the Liberty Bell and Independence Hall speak resonantly of the nation's birth. Each city tells its own unique story, making it a living museum of cultural heritage that is both educational and exhilarating.

Accessing these historical treasures is key to ensuring everyone can enjoy their splendors. Museums and cultural institutions across these cities have made significant strides in accommodating visitors with diverse needs. From wheelchair-accessible entrances and tactile exhibits for the visually impaired to hearing loops for the hearing impaired, these facilities are designed to ensure the richness of American history is available to all. For instance, the Smithsonian Museums in Washington, D.C., offer various accessibility services, including sign language interpretation and morning tours for visitors with cognitive and sensory processing disabilities.

Consider joining a local tour designed for seniors for a more structured exploration. These tours are paced to be leisurely and thorough, with knowledgeable guides who bring the history and architecture of these cities to life. In San Francisco, for instance, you can join tours that explore the iconic Golden Gate Bridge and historic Fisherman's Wharf, where the past meets the present in colorful, lively displays. These tours provide deeper insights into the city's heritage and cater to comfort, often including rest stops and places to relax and soak in the surroundings.

A cultural deep-dive would only be complete with indulging in the local culinary traditions. American cities are melting pots of flavors, each with its signature dishes that tell the story of the people and the influences that have shaped them. In New Orleans, you can savor the spicy notes of Creole cuisine on a food tour that takes you from venerable eateries to hidden gems. Or, in New York City, sample the legendary delicacies of the Lower East Side, from bagels to knishes, each bite a testament to the immigrant stories woven into the city's culinary DNA. Many cities also offer cooking classes that focus on regional specialties. There's nothing quite like learning to make authentic clam chowder in a Boston kitchen under the guidance of a local chef.

As you immerse yourself in these cultural experiences, remember that each moment spent in these historic cities adds a rich layer to your life story. The architecture, the sounds, the flavors, and the tales of yore educate and entertain us and connect us more deeply to the places we visit. They transform our travels from mere sightseeing to meaningful engagements with the past and present of our vibrant American landscape.

In wrapping up our exploration of America's historic cities, we've journeyed through time via the historic streets of Boston, experienced the vibrant culture of New Orleans, and tasted the diverse flavors of cities like Charleston and San Francisco. With its unique heritage and offerings, each city has provided us with more than just knowledge; they've enriched our lives with experiences that resonate deeply and personally. As we wrap up this chapter, we leave with more than just memories of these cultural experiences—we deeply appreciate America's rich history and traditions. Looking ahead, we continue our exploration of unique travel experiences, ready to discover more treasures that await in our beautiful and diverse country.

The Ultimate Senior Travel Guide

TAILORED AND PRACTICAL ADVICE, INSPIRATION FOR NEW ADVENTURES, COMPREHENSIVE PLANNING TOOLS, AND ENHANCED TRAVEL EXPERIENCE

"Travel is the only thing you buy that makes you richer." - Anonymous

Hey there! I'm Pauline Winslow, your guide on this exciting journey of senior travel. Not too long ago, I was in your shoes—curious yet overwhelmed by the idea of traveling in my golden years. But as I ventured out, my apprehension turned into pure joy, and travel became my passion. My mission is to make travel accessible and enjoyable for all seniors.

I know what you might think: "Is it possible for me to travel comfortably and safely at my age?" Let's tackle those fears together. With the right advice, tools, and tips, you can have stress-free, enriching travel experiences. That's what "The Ultimate Senior Travel Guide" is all about.

To help make this guide even better, I have a question for you...

Would you help a fellow senior traveler, even if you never got credit for it?

Who is this person you ask? They are like you. Or, at least, like you used to be. Curious about travel, wanting to explore new places, and needing help figuring out where to start.

Our mission is to make senior travel accessible to everyone. Everything I do stems from that mission, and the only way to accomplish it is to reach... everyone.

This is where you come in. Most people judge a book by its cover (and its reviews). So here's my ask for those travelers you've never met: Please help those travelers by leaving this book a review.

Your gift costs no money and takes less than 60 seconds to make real, but it can change a fellow senior traveler's life forever. Your review could help...

- One more senior traveler explores the world with confidence.
- One more retiree finds joy and excitement in new adventures.
- One more couple creates lasting memories together.
- One more solo traveler feels safe and inspired on their journey.
- One more person fulfills their travel dreams.

To get that "feel good" feeling and help this person for real, you only have to leave a review, which takes less than 60 seconds.

Simply scan the QR code below to leave your review:

If you enjoy helping others, you're exactly who I'm looking to connect with. Welcome to the community! I'm excited to help you navigate your travel journey and can't wait to share more tips and strategies in the coming chapters.

Thank you from the bottom of my heart. Now, back to our regularly scheduled programming.

Your biggest fan,

Pauline Winslow

P.S. Sharing valuable advice makes you a key part of someone else's journey. Please pass this book on if you believe it will benefit another traveler.

NINE

City Breaks and Rural Escapes

Imagine slipping into the leisurely rhythm of a European city where the days unfold with the grace of a leisurely waltz, not the frantic tempo of a weekday morning commute. Here, in the old heart of Europe, cities have perfected the art of slow living—where café seats invite you to linger over a second cup of coffee and museum halls whisper stories of ages past. It's a place where history mingles seamlessly with the present, offering a travel experience that feels both timeless and invitingly slow. Welcome to the chapter where we explore European cities that are not just stops on a map but pauses in time—perfect for those who prefer to savor each moment.

European Cities with a Slow Pace

Charming Cities

Let's meander through the streets of some of Europe's most charming cities, where the pace of life takes a stroll rather than a sprint. Consider Ljubljana, Slovenia's enchanting capital, where car traffic is restricted in the city center, paving the way for pedestrians and cyclists to explore at their own pace. The city's café culture encourages sitting back and enjoying the view of the Ljubljanica River, bordered by outdoor book markets and street artists. Then there's Bruges, in Belgium, where medieval architecture and winding canals set the scene for slow exploration on foot or by boat. With their historic belfries, the market squares invite you to step back in time and relax into the rhythm of this picturesque city.

Accessible Attractions

These cities aren't just about charm; they're also accessibility champions. Many of Europe's slower-paced cities have become very mindful of accessibility, making them perfect for senior travelers. In Vienna, for example, the major museums offer not only wheelchair access but also guided tours designed to be senior-friendly, involving minimal walking and plenty of opportunities to sit and discuss the art. The city's trams and buses have low entry points, making public transportation a breeze for those with mobility issues. Similarly, Porto's historic sites, like the famous Lello Bookstore, now offer elevators and ramps, ensuring everyone can explore the city's cultural riches without concern.

Local Living Experiences

For a truly immersive experience, why not consider living like a local? Many European cities known for their slow pace offer short-term apartment rentals that allow you to settle in and experience the city from a resident's perspective. Living in a pedestrian-friendly neighborhood in cities like Florence and Seville allows you to explore local markets, quaint cafes, and neighborhood galleries at your leisure while having a home base that feels like your own. Participating in local life also means embracing the local market culture—places like the Naschmarkt in Vienna or the Mercado de San Miguel in Madrid are not just spots to grab fresh produce but are also social hubs where locals meet, chat, and enjoy the day.

Transportation Tips

Navigating the streets of Europe's more relaxed cities can be an adventure, but it doesn't have to be daunting. Most of these cities offer senior-friendly public transportation options. For instance, trams in Prague have dedicated spaces for those with limited mobility, and their frequent service means you never have to rush to catch one. Many cities also offer cards like the Berlin WelcomeCard or the Amsterdam City Card, which provide unlimited public transport and discounts at many attractions, making them perfect for the senior traveler looking to explore at their own pace.

In these slower-paced European cities, every alley whispers stories, every square invites pause, and life's rhythm encourages you to take your time, breathe it all in, and let the history and beauty of the place wash over you. Whether it's through the lens of accessible cultural sites, the coziness of a local apartment, or the convenience of senior-friendly transport, these cities offer a travel experience that says, 'Why rush?'—after all, the beauty of travel lies as much in the journey as in the destination.

Rural Retreats in New Zealand and Australia

Imagine the soft hum of nature, the wide, colorful sky above you, and landscapes that tell stories of ancient times and hidden wonders. This is the heart of the rural retreats in New Zealand and Australia, where the serene beauty of nature isn't just viewed but deeply felt. Picture yourself in the rolling vineyards of the Barossa Valley, where the earth itself seems infused with the spirit of the old vines, or find yourself standing by the majestic fjords of Milford Sound in New Zealand, where waterfalls cascade down sheer cliffs into pristine waters below. These destinations offer more than just a break from the urban hustle; they offer a sanctuary where the soul can breathe, and the heart can roam free.

For those looking to relax and enjoy some light exploration, the rural areas of New Zealand and Australia are perfect natural playgrounds. Consider the experience of a hot air balloon ride at dawn over the Yarra Valley, where the world below awakens in hues of amber and gold, or a scenic rail journey through the mystical landscapes of New Zealand's South Island, where every turn presents a postcard-worthy view. These activities offer the thrill of discovery at a pace that respects both your sense of adventure and your preference for comfort. Moreover, spa retreats nestled in these natural settings, like those in Daylesford, Australia, or Hanmer Springs in New Zealand, provide a perfect blend of natural beauty and pampering, offering treatments that utilize local minerals and plants known for their healing properties.

Delving deeper into the cultural fabric of these regions, rural retreats offer profound insights into the indigenous heritage that shapes both the landscape and the people of New Zealand and Australia. In New Zealand, experiencing Māori culture through storytelling sessions that share the land's legends or traditional ceremonies like the pōwhiri (welcome ceremony) enhances your understanding of this beautiful country and its people. In Australia, experiences like walking tours with Aboriginal guides offer a unique perspective on the land known as Australia's Red Centre, sharing ancient stories and traditions that highlight the deep connection between the Indigenous people and the land. These cultural encounters are not just educational; they are transformative, offering a window into the soul of these nations.

Accommodations in these rural retreats are thoughtfully designed to ensure that comfort is paramount. In New Zealand, lodges and cottages often feature single-level layouts, minimizing the need for stairs and making it easier to enjoy your stay without concern for mobility issues. Many of these accommodations are strategically located to offer stunning views of the surrounding landscapes, ensuring that nature is always a glance away. In Australia, rural accommodations frequently offer on-site dining options that source ingredients locally, bringing the region's taste directly to your table. These retreats cater to your comfort and strive to make your stay as seamless and enjoyable as possible, with staff ready to assist with planning day trips or arranging transportation to nearby attractions.

Exploring the rural retreats of New Zealand and Australia allows you to step into a world where the pace slows, the air clears, and the beauty of the earth unfolds in all its breathtaking splendor. Here, the balance between the land, culture, and relaxation is part of every experience, inviting you to connect deeply with the beautiful landscapes and rich heritage of these remarkable destinations. Whether you find yourself sipping a glass of fine wine as the sun sets over a vineyard or listening to the hauntingly beautiful sounds of a didgeridoo under a starlit sky, these rural escapes offer a profound reminder of the joys of exploring at your own pace, with the earth's beauty as your constant companion.

The Allure of Asian Metropolises

Step into the bustling streets of Tokyo, Singapore, and Seoul, and you'll find cities pulsating with a rhythm that blends the old with the new in a dazzling dance of culture and innovation. These metropolises, with their neon lights and towering skyscrapers, also hold serene spots where tradition breathes and thrives. These cities offer a vibrant tableau for the senior traveler, rich with experiences catering to the energetic and those seeking a more measured pace.

The vibrant city life in these Asian giants blends history and modernity. In Tokyo, ancient temples quietly stand among the hustle and bustle of a super-modern city. Here, you can witness the serene ritual of a tea ceremony just a short metro ride away from the bustling Shibuya Crossing. Similarly, Singapore offers a blend of lush, verdant gardens and cutting-edge architecture, embodying a forward-looking spirit rooted in deep cultural heritage. The city's Botanic Gardens, a UNESCO World Heritage site, provide a tranquil refuge from the urban rush. With its palatial residences and contemporary art scenes, Seoul invites you to stroll through history at the Gyeongbokgung Palace before enjoying the artistic innovations at the Dongdaemun Design Plaza.

For senior travelers, these cities are not just accessible but welcoming, with numerous attractions that cater to those who favor a leisurely pace. In Tokyo, the historic Asakusa district, centered around the Senso-ji Temple, offers a glimpse into the city's past with streets that are easy to navigate and lined with stalls offering traditional wares and snacks. Singapore's Gardens by the Bay is a marvel of garden design and is fully accessible, allowing you to explore its floral splendor easily. In Seoul, the Insadong neighborhood is a cultural feast that is largely pedestrian-friendly and known for its antique shops and tea houses, where you can savor traditional Korean teas and sweets.

Navigating these cities is made simpler by their efficient public transportation systems. Tokyo's rail and subway networks are models of punctuality and accessibility, with clear signage in multiple languages and dedicated seating for seniors and people with disabilities. Singapore's Mass Rapid Transit (MRT) system offers smooth, barrier-free travel throughout the city-state, with tactile paving for the visually impaired and wide gates for wheelchair users. Seoul's subway system, similarly, is equipped with lifts, ramps, and tactile guides, making it remarkably senior-friendly. Each city also offers travel cards that can be used across various modes of public transport, simplifying travel and reducing the need to manage multiple tickets.

Engaging in the cultural offerings of these cities provides a deeper connection to their essence. Participate in a tea ceremony in Tokyo, where the meticulous preparation and serene setting offer a meditative respite from the city's hustle. In Singapore, join a cultural workshop to learn traditional crafts such as batik painting, offering a creative outlet and a tangible connection to the region's artistic heritage. Seoul's vibrant performance arts scene welcomes you to experience traditional music and dance performances that are entertaining and rich in cultural storytelling.

These Asian cities, with their mix of old and new, offer senior travelers a variety of experiences that are both easy to access and deeply engaging. From the quiet corners of historic temples to the vibrant throngs of modern city centers, these cities invite you to explore at your own pace, offering a journey that is as comfortable as it is captivating.

In exploring city breaks and rural escapes, we've journeyed through the slow-paced European cities rich in charm and accessibility, ventured into the tranquil rural retreats of New Zealand and Australia, and immersed ourselves in the vibrant life of Asian metropolises. Each destination, with its unique offerings, ensures that the senior traveler can find both adventure and comfort, from the serene landscapes of the countryside to the bustling streets of the world's most dynamic cities. As we wrap up this chapter, we take a collection of memorable experiences, ready to dive into the next adventure. The upcoming chapters promise even more discoveries and joys in travel.

TEN

Active Adventures and Wellness

Who says adventure has an age limit? Certainly not us! As we dive into the rejuvenating world of active adventures, we leave stereotypes at the door and lace up our walking shoes for truly enriching experiences. My dear friends, walking tours are not merely about stretching the legs but also about enriching the soul and sharpening the mind. So, whether you're meandering through medieval streets, exploring lush gardens, or strolling along riverbanks, these walking adventures are your ticket to a healthier, happier you.

Walking Tours Tailored for Seniors

Gentle Exploration

Imagine embarking on a walking tour designed with your comfort and interests at heart. These aren't your average rushed city tours but thoughtful, well-paced excursions that respect your rhythm and cater to your curiosity. Picture walking tours through the lavender fields of Provence, where the path is as smooth as the breeze is scented, or a gentle stroll around the historic heart of Prague, with plenty of benches to rest and soak in the Gothic architecture. These tours are crafted to ensure they are accessible, often with flat paths and plenty of spots to rest, making them perfect for those with mobility aids.

Tour operators specializing in senior travel are increasingly mindful of including routes that minimize physical strain without compromising the richness of the experience. They often offer personal audio systems so you can hear your guide clearly without staying in a tight group, allowing you to wander if something catches your eye. Plus, with smaller groups, you don't have to jostle for the best spot or rush through a site because the group needs to move on. It's all about savoring the moment, one step at a time.

Cultural Richness

These walking tours are gateways to cultural immersion. They are thoughtfully intertwined with the culture and history of the places they explore, turning every corner into a story and every street into a chapter of history. In cities like Florence or Istanbul, where every stone is steeped in history, these tours help you connect the dots between the past and the present. Guides, often locals, share facts, personal stories, and insights that guidebooks gloss over.

Imagine stopping by a small, family-owned pastry shop in Lisbon during your walk, tasting a traditional Pastel de Nata. At the same time, your guide tells you about the neighborhood's transformation over the decades. Or perhaps, while wandering through a market in Marrakech, you learn from your guide the best spices to buy - not just for your cooking but for your health. These experiences enrich your travel and deepen your understanding of diverse cultures, all at a pace that lets you truly absorb and reflect on what you're learning.

Health Benefits

Let's talk about the heart of the matter—quite literally! Walking is a fantastic cardiovascular exercise known for improving heart health, reducing the risk of hypertension, and enhancing overall stamina. But the benefits of these walking tours go beyond the physical. They are a boon for mental health, providing a change of scenery that can boost mood and alleviate symptoms of depression and anxiety. Combining fresh air, social interaction, and mental stimulation from learning about new places significantly enhances cognitive function and emotional well-being.

Walking also fosters social interactions, which are crucial as we age. These tours often lead to new friendships as you share experiences and stories with fellow walkers. The shared joy of discovery creates bonds that can turn a group of strangers into a group of travel companions, sometimes even lifelong friends.

Safety Tips

While the allure of adventure is strong, safety always walks alongside. Here are a few tips to ensure your walking tours are as safe as they are enjoyable:

- Appropriate Footwear: Wear sturdy, comfortable shoes with good support and slip resistance. Your feet will thank you after a day of exploring.
- Stay Hydrated: Keep a water bottle handy.

Dehydration can sneak up on you, especially in warmer climates or during summer months.
- Sun Protection: Always wear sunscreen, a hat, and sunglasses. Even on cloudy days, UV rays can be strong, especially in cities near the water where reflection increases exposure.
- Know Your Limits: Listen to your body. If you need to rest, don't hesitate to let your guide know or to sit out a part of the tour. Remember, it's about enjoyment, not endurance.

Walking tours for seniors are about maintaining physical fitness and enriching life with new experiences, learning, and connections. They remind us that at any age, the world is ours to explore at our own pace, with curiosity and joy leading the way. So, tie up those laces, pick up that walking stick, and step out into a world brimming with stories waiting to be walked through. Who knows what discoveries lie just around the next bend?

Yoga Retreats and Wellness Sanctuaries Worldwide

Imagine a serene morning, the sun gently rising over a lush landscape, birds chirping in the background, and you, on a mat, taking a deep breath of fresh, clean air, surrounded by nature and tranquility. What if I told you this could be your reality, not just a daydream? Welcome to the world of yoga retreats and wellness sanctuaries, perfect for seasoned citizens looking to blend relaxation with rejuvenation. These havens of health are not about twisting yourself into a pretzel but finding a new zest for life through practices that enrich both body and mind.

Let's take a virtual trip to some of the most serene spots on the planet where wellness isn't just a program but a way of life. Picture the tranquil ashrams of India, where yoga is as much a part of the landscape as the Ganges. These places offer more than just yoga; they provide a spiritual journey that marries ancient practices with the wisdom of age. Or, perhaps the laid-back, pura vida lifestyle of Costa Rica's sandy beaches is more your speed, where eco-friendly wellness resorts nestle between the jungle and the sea, offering a blend of yoga, meditation, and nature therapy. These sanctuaries are designed with the understanding that peace comes not just from our actions but from our surroundings. They're located where the environment contributes to healing—think vast mountain vistas, tranquil beaches, and lush forests, all as soothing to the spirit as a cool breeze on a hot day.

Now, not all of us can bend like we used to, and that's perfectly fine because the beauty of yoga at these retreats is its adaptability. Many places offer forms of yoga and wellness activities tailored just for seniors. Chair yoga, for instance, is fantastic for those who might find traditional poses challenging. Then there's water therapy, which uses water's buoyancy to ease joint strain while you get a good stretch. And let's not forget about meditation and guided relaxation practices, which are great for the mind and can be done by just about anyone, regardless of physical flexibility. These programs are not about pushing your limits but gently expanding them, enhancing your physical and mental well-being in a supportive and nurturing environment.

The community aspect of these retreats is something special, too. You're not just a visitor; you become part of a community of like-minded souls, all there to support and uplift each other.

It's wonderful how a shared session of sunrise yoga or a group meditation can lead to friendships that enrich our lives long after we've rolled up our mats. These retreats often include communal meals of nutritious, thoughtfully prepared food, where conversations flow as freely as herbal tea. It's about connecting, sharing experiences, and learning from each other in a setting that fosters community and togetherness.

So, whether you want to deepen your yoga practice or spend a week being pampered and rejuvenated in a beautiful setting, there's a yoga retreat or wellness sanctuary. It's more than just a holiday; it's an investment in your health, a way to recharge your batteries, and maybe even discover a new passion. After all, trying something new is never too late, especially when it promises to bring more balance, peace, and happiness into your life. So why not treat yourself to a retreat? Your body, mind, and spirit will thank you for it.

Cycling Tours for Every Level of Experience

Imagine the gentle breeze against your face as you pedal along a scenic route, surrounded by stunning landscapes that unfold like a live painting with every turn. Cycling tours offer this delightful experience and believe me, they cater wonderfully to seniors who wish to combine the joy of exploration with the benefits of staying active. These tours are designed to accommodate varying levels of cycling experience, ensuring that everyone from the novice to the seasoned cyclist finds their stride and enjoys the ride.

Scenic routes are the heart of these cycling tours. Picture yourself cycling through the vineyards of Tuscany, where every pedal stroke takes you past rows of grapevines and opens up views to ancient hilltop towns. Or, consider a leisurely ride along the Danube River, where the paths are as flat as they are picturesque, making it easy to soak in the sights without breaking a sweat. Electric bikes (e-bikes) are a fantastic option, providing enough assistance to help you tackle a hill or extend your range without compromising the enjoyment of the ride. These e-bikes are easy to handle and can be adjusted to provide varying levels of assistance, making them perfect for seniors who love exploring on two wheels but prefer to exert only a little energy.

Cycling tours also offer a unique form of cultural immersion. These aren't just about the physical act of cycling; they're about what you see, whom you meet, and what you learn along the way. They allow you to access unreachable places by coach tours or walking. Imagine pedaling through a remote village in Vietnam, stopping to chat with local artisans, or cycling to a hidden beach in Greece that only locals know about. These experiences provide a deeper connection to the places you visit, turning a simple ride into a journey of cultural discovery. Guides on these tours are often locals who provide insights into the history and culture of the area, adding layers of meaning to the sights you pass, from historical landmarks to local markets.

Now, let's talk about the support you get on these tours. Operators are incredibly mindful of the needs of senior cyclists. Support vehicles accompany most tours, ready to assist anyone who needs a break or encounters a mechanical issue. Bikes provided on these tours are chosen for their comfort and reliability, with options available for different heights and preferences. Helmets, high-visibility vests, and water bottles are typically provided, ensuring safety and comfort throughout the ride. Additionally, the guides are trained to pace the group according to its abilities, often splitting groups based on speed preferences. This means you can take your time and enjoy the ride at a pace that suits you without feeling pressured to keep up.

The health benefits of cycling, especially at a senior-friendly pace, cannot be overstated. It's a wonderful way to improve cardiovascular fitness and enhance leg strength while being gentle on the joints compared to higher-impact activities. Moreover, the rhythmic nature of cycling can be quite meditative, providing mental benefits such as reduced anxiety and improved mood. The social aspect of these tours—sharing the experience with others, enjoying group lunches, and celebrating the day's ride—adds a layer of emotional well-being, turning each tour into an opportunity for making new friends and sharing joyful moments.

In wrapping up our exploration of cycling tours, remember that these experiences are designed to be enjoyable, accessible, and enriching. They're about taking in the world's beauty at your own pace, with all the support you need to make your ride comfortable and enjoyable. So why not saddle up and see where the path leads? You might find that cycling is your new favorite way to eAs we pedal forward from the rolling hills and quiet trails of our cycling adventures, we gear up for our next chapter, where we'll unpack the essentials of smart and safe travel—ensuring that your trips are as smooth as they are enjoyable. Stay tuned for practical tips that make every trip a breeze, from packing smart to confidently navigating new destinations.

ELEVEN

Cultural Immersion and Educational Journeys

Ah, the sweet sound of "Bonjour" or perhaps "Buongiorno!" rings differently when you're standing under the Eiffel Tower or navigating the quaint cobblestone alleys of Rome, right? Welcome to the enchanting realm of language learning holidays, a delightful fusion of vacation and education, where the classroom walls dissolve into the landscapes of countries that speak the language you're eager to learn. Picture this: you're not just learning Spanish; you're ordering tapas in a bustling Barcelona café, practicing your new skills with the friendly waiter. This chapter is your gateway to turning language barriers into bridges, connecting you directly with new cultures, people, and experiences.

Language Learning Holidays

Language Immersion

Think of language learning holidays as a deep dive into a language and a culture. The concept is brilliantly simple yet profoundly impactful. You travel to a country where the language you wish to learn is spoken natively and immerse yourself in everyday communication. This isn't about cramming grammar or sweating over vocabulary in a stifling classroom. It's about lively, practical engagement with the language, where every street sign, menu, and conversation is part of your learning experience. Imagine bargaining at a local market in Marrakech in Arabic or discussing history with a group of locals at a café in Vienna. Each interaction is a mini-lesson in language and cultural nuances that textbooks can't convey.

Senior-Friendly Programs

If stepping into a typical language class with multitudes of younger students sounds intimidating, fear not! Numerous language schools and programs across the globe are tailored specifically for mature learners like you. These programs understand that you might appreciate a slightly slower pace, more repetition, or more context. They combine language learning with cultural outings—such as guided museum tours, historical walks, or theater visits—making learning enjoyable and deeply immersive. Schools such as the Tandem Madrid or Institut de Français offer classes that focus on practical conversational skills, set in supportive and engaging environments. These aren't just lessons; they're gateways to new experiences crafted to keep you engaged and motivated.

Cognitive Benefits

The perks of learning a new language stretch far beyond being able to ask for directions to the nearest museum. For seniors, engaging in language education can be a potent tool against cognitive decline. It's like a gym workout for your brain, challenging you to recognize, recall, and negotiate meaning in new ways. Studies show that bilingualism can delay the onset of dementia and significantly improve focus and memory. Every new word or grammatical structure you master is not just a tick on your language checklist; it boosts your brain health, enhancing cognitive flexibility and problem-solving skills. What is the joy of mastering a conversation in a foreign language? Exhilarating!

Social Interactions

The social dimension is one of the most beautiful aspects of these language holidays. You'll be learning alongside fellow language enthusiasts, many of whom are also seniors, sharing the same eagerness to explore and understand new cultures. These settings foster friendships and provide a supportive network of peers who encourage each other's progress. Beyond the classroom, engaging with local communities allows you to practice your new skills in real-life situations—chatting with local craftsmen, making friends in the park, or sharing stories with new acquaintances. Each interaction improves your language skills and connects you more deeply to the social and cultural life of the place you're visiting.

Interactive Element: Language Challenge Journal

To enrich your language learning journey, keep a 'Language Challenge Journal.' Each day, jot down new words, phrases, or conversations you have had. Reflect on these entries and note any cultural insights gained. This journal can become a cherished keepsake of your travels, a tangible record of your linguistic and cultural adventures.

Embarking on a language-learning holiday is like opening the door to a new dimension of travel experiences. It's about embracing the challenge of learning, the joy of connecting, and the thrill of discovering the world through the lens of another language. So, dust off your phrasebooks, pack your curiosity, and prepare to expand your horizons in the most engaging way possible.

Volunteer Opportunities Abroad: Giving Back While Traveling

Think about the last time you felt wholly fulfilled. Was it while you were giving something back to the community? If that rings true, you might find deep satisfaction in volunteer opportunities abroad, where giving extends beyond borders and touches lives meaningfully. Imagine yourself teaching English to eager young minds in a small village in Thailand or helping with wildlife conservation efforts in the lush rainforests of Costa Rica. These experiences allow you to contribute positively while absorbing new cultures and landscapes. It's about making a difference, one day at a time, in a setting that's as enriching for you as it is for those you help.

Choosing the right volunteer program is crucial—like finding a shoe that fits just right. It needs to match your skills and interests but also accommodate your physical capabilities, ensuring the experience is rewarding and not draining. Many organizations cater specifically to senior volunteers, offering roles that leverage the wealth of experience and wisdom that comes with age without requiring you to perform physically strenuous tasks. For instance, you could engage in community education programs, assist with local art projects, or help small business owners develop better marketing strategies. These programs utilize your skills and respect your physical comfort levels.

The beauty of volunteering abroad lies in the rich cultural exchange that occurs. It's a two-way street; you get to immerse yourself in the local way of life, understand the nuances of their traditions and daily challenges, and share insights from your life experiences. This exchange fosters a deeper understanding and appreciation of cultural diversity, enriching your travel experience beyond typical tourist interactions. Picture sharing a meal with a local family, where you learn about their customs and daily life, and in return, you share stories from your own culture, creating a beautiful blend of knowledge and mutual respect.

Preparing for such a travel adventure takes thoughtful consideration, especially regarding health and safety. Ensure you're up to date with any necessary vaccinations and have adequate health insurance coverage. It's also wise to familiarize yourself with the cultural norms and legal requirements of the country you're visiting to avoid any cultural faux pas or legal issues. The volunteer organization typically provides safety training and emergency preparedness, but being proactive is always good. Learn a few phrases in the local language, understand how to seek help if needed, and always have a way to contact your program coordinators in an emergency.

Volunteering abroad in your golden years can be one of the most fulfilling experiences. It offers a unique blend of travel, cultural immersion, and the joy of giving back. It's about leaving a positive imprint on the places you visit, not just with your work but with the stories and experiences you share. So, pack your bags with essentials, compassion, and a readiness to learn and help. The world is vast, and its opportunities for meaningful connections are endless.

Cooking Classes and Wine-Tasting Tours

Imagine yourself in a cozy, sunlit kitchen in Tuscany, surrounded by the fresh aromas of basil and ripe tomatoes, learning to make authentic Italian marinara sauce from a local chef whose family has lived in the region for generations. Or you envision yourself in the rolling hills of Napa Valley, sipping a finely aged Cabernet as you learn about the subtleties of oak and tannins from a seasoned vintner. Cooking classes and wine-tasting tours provide enriching experiences beyond the simple enjoyment of food and drink; they immerse you in the local culture, teach you new skills, and offer a chance to connect with fellow enthusiasts over shared tastes and stories.

In these cooking classes, you don't just follow recipes; you dive into the culinary traditions of the region, guided by chefs who are often as passionate about teaching as they are about cooking. These classes are designed to be accessible regardless of your culinary background. Whether you're learning to roll sushi in Japan or knead dough for the perfect French baguette, the emphasis is on fun, learning, and participation. You'll discover local ingredients—perhaps some you've never heard of—and learn techniques chefs use to create flavors that dance on the palate. More than just a meal, each dish you prepare is a story about the people, history, and geography of the place you're visiting.

Wine-tasting tours, on the other hand, offer an equally engaging but more relaxed experience. These tours take you through beautiful vineyards, where the grapes hang heavy on the vine, and into cellars, where the air is cool and filled with aging wine. Here, you're not just a tourist but a viticulture student learning about the process from grape to glass. Wine experts share their knowledge of different grape varieties, fermentation processes, and aging techniques, culminating in the art of wine tasting. You'll learn how to note the nuances of color, aroma, and flavor and how to pair wine perfectly with food.

The social dining experiences often accompanying cooking classes and wine tours are a highlight for many. Picture a long table set under the open sky, candles flickering as dusk falls, with people from all walks of life gathered around. There's laughter, stories being exchanged, and glasses clinking to celebrate the meal everyone helped prepare. These moments are about more than just eating; they're about forging connections, sharing joy and creating memories long after the last bite is savored.

But while enjoying everything, it's important to remember to stay balanced, especially for your health and well-being. These culinary experiences cater to your dietary needs and preferences, ensuring you can enjoy the delicious offerings without compromise. Chefs and tour guides are typically very accommodating and able to adjust recipes and menus for low-sodium, low-sugar, or gluten-free options, ensuring that everyone can partake fully and healthily.

Cooking classes and wine-tasting tours blend education, social interaction, and sensory delight, offering a fulfilling way to understand and appreciate new cultures through their flavors. These experiences invite you to slow down, savor each moment, and soak in the joys of food and drink made all the richer by the stories they tell and the people you share them with. So, whether you're a seasoned gourmand or a curious foodie, these culinary journeys add a flavorful layer to your travel adventures, enriching your understanding of the world one bite, one sip, at a time.

As we close this delicious chapter on culinary and wine adventures, we've stirred our way through cooking classes that open windows to cultural traditions and sipped our way through vineyards that offer a taste of the local heritage. Each experience is a step deeper into the heart of the places we visit through the universal language of food and drink. Looking ahead, we continue exploring enriching travel experiences, ready to unveil more ways to engage deeply and joyfully with the world around us. Let's carry the zest and flavor from our culinary adventures into all the journeys that await in the coming chapters.

TWELVE

Documenting Your Travels

Ah, the art of capturing the essence of your travels, not just in souvenirs or stories told over dinner tables, but in vibrant, vivid photographs that speak a thousand words per pixel. Think of your camera as your trusty sidekick, always ready to freeze a moment in time, from the grandeur of a sunset over the Sahara to the sparkling eyes of a street vendor in Bangkok. Whether you're a snap-happy amateur or a seasoned shutterbug, this chapter guides you to ensure those golden travel memories are beautifully preserved, easily accessible, and joyfully shared.

Travel Photography Tips

Capturing Moments

Let's dive right into the heart of travel photography—capturing those moments that make your heart skip a beat. Choosing the right camera is crucial; it's like picking a dance partner who steps in sync with your rhythm. For seniors, the best camera is one that balances simplicity with quality. Lightweight models with automatic settings and a good zoom can work wonders without the fuss. Brands like Canon and Nikon offer user-friendly cameras that provide excellent image quality without needing to fiddle with too many settings.

Mastering a few basic techniques can elevate your photos from nice snapshots to stunning galleries of your adventures. Composition is key—try the 'rule of thirds,' where you imagine your screen divided into a grid of nine equal segments and place the subject of your photo along these lines or their intersections. This technique helps in capturing photos that are naturally pleasing to the eye. Also, don't shy away from capturing the essence of the locale through its people and their daily lives. A photo of a local fisherman repairing his net on a Vietnamese boat tells a richer story than a generic shoreline shot.

Memory Preservation

Photography is a powerful tool for memory preservation, enabling you to capture experiences as vividly as you lived them. But it's not just about landscapes and landmarks. The true flavor of your travels often lies in the in-between moments: a cup of coffee at a Parisian café, the laughter of children playing in a Moroccan medina, the serene old couple walking hand in hand through Central Park. These images become priceless archives of your journey, evoking emotions and stories every time you revisit them.

Technology Simplified

Navigating the world of photography technology can be manageable. For seniors looking to enhance their photos without getting bogged down by complex editing software, there are user-friendly apps that can make a world of difference. Apps like Snapseed or Adobe Photoshop Express offer intuitive interfaces that allow you to enhance colors, crop images, and even remove unwanted elements with simple taps and swipes. These tools can help refine your photos to reflect your experiences' beauty better.

Sharing and Storage

Once you've captured and polished your memories, sharing them becomes part of the joy of travel. Platforms like Google Photos or iCloud Photos offer secure cloud storage to keep your photos safe and make it easy to create albums and share them with friends and family via email or social media. Consider creating photo books through services like Shutterfly or Blurb for a more tangible touch. These books can be wonderful gifts and keepsakes, turning your travel adventures into beautifully bound stories to be enjoyed by generations to come.

Interactive Element: Photo Enhancement Tutorial

To help you get the most out of your travel photographs, here's a quick tutorial on using a simple photo editing app to enhance your images:

1. **Open your photos in the app**: Choose an image that captures a memorable moment from your travels.
2. **Adjust the brightness and contrast**: Brighten the photo if it's too dark, and adjust the contrast to make the colors pop.

3. **Crop for composition**: Use the thirds grid rule to crop your photo, positioning key elements along the grid lines.
4. **Apply a filter**: Experiment with filters to find one that enhances the mood of your photo.
5. **Save and share**: Save the edited photo and consider sharing it with friends or including it in a digital album.

This tutorial can be a fun exercise to bring your travel photos to life, making them as vibrant and enduring as your memories. Whether you're sharing these photos online or flipping through them in a photo book, each image serves as a vivid bookmark in the story of your adventures, ready to transport you back to those cherished moments with just a glance.

Keeping a Travel Journal: Capturing Memories in Words

Ah, the humble journal—your repository of thoughts, observations, and those quirky little anecdotes that a camera can't capture. Imagine sitting under the shade of a sprawling oak in a Tuscan vineyard, pen in hand, journal on your lap, scribbling away the day's escapades. This isn't just about chronicling what you saw; it's about engraving your emotional journey onto paper, where every word serves as a brushstroke, painting your unique travel narrative. Whether you're experienced at keeping a journal or just starting, writing about your travels can turn your trips into a collection of meaningful experiences. Your words will bring memories to life, even years later.

Now, consider the therapeutic rhythm of writing—the scratch of pen on paper, the flow of ink as you detail a particularly vibrant sunset or the smile of a street vendor who shared an apple with you. Writing can be meditative, a quiet moment of reflection that allows you to digest the day's experiences and serves as a mindfulness exercise. It calms the mind, soothes the soul, and offers a precious pause in the often hectic pace of travel. More than just a memory aid, your journal becomes a private space where writing helps distill the essence of your experiences, making them even more meaningful.

Embracing creativity in your journaling can add a delightful dimension to this practice. Who says it has to be all words? Perhaps sketches of the Eiffel Tower can be seen from a cozy café or watercolor dabs reflecting the azure blues of Santorini. Or why not a bit of scrapbooking? Imagine pasting a ticket stub from that unforgettable Broadway show or a dried leaf from the trail you conquered in the Rockies. Each journal page can become a canvas, a mixed-media masterpiece that captures the textures of your travels. This creative liberty enhances the enjoyment of journaling and makes each entry vividly personal and immensely fun.

Let's inspire those pages with a few prompts and ideas. How about describing a day entirely through your senses? What did the morning coffee smell like in Brazil, how did the silk of a sari in India feel, or what was the muezzin's call in Istanbul at dusk? Or reflect on a conversation with a local that offered you a new perspective; what did you learn, and how did it change your view of the world? Maybe jot down a funny incident, like when you tried to order a meal in Italian and ended up with something completely unexpected. These prompts are your starting blocks; from there, let your thoughts run free, capturing the essence of your journey one word at a time.

Lastly, consider the legacy of your travel journals. These are personal keepsakes and potential heirlooms that can be passed down, offering your progeny or even friends a window into your world. They'll travel alongside you through your words, experiencing the sights, sounds, and souls of places they may never visit. Your journals can serve as a bridge across generations, a shared family treasure that keeps your adventurous spirit alive and inspires others long after your travels have ended. They are a testament to a well-traveled, well-lived, and well-loved life. So, grab that journal and start writing; your future self—and perhaps future generations—will thank you.

Blogging Your Journey: Sharing Stories with Loved Ones

Step into the digital age where storytelling morphs into blogging, a fantastic highway that connects your travel escapades with the world in just a few clicks. Imagine this: your experiences, from the bustling markets of Marrakech to the serene beaches of Bali, are no longer confined to your memory or the ears of your close ones; they're available for the world to see and read. Blogging isn't just about writing; it's about sharing your journey personally and universally, turning every reader into a virtual travel companion.

Starting a blog might sound like treading into tech-savvy territory, but it's remarkably senior-friendly. Begin by choosing a blogging platform that resonates with your tech comfort level. Platforms like WordPress and Blogger offer user-friendly interfaces that don't require you to be a tech wizard. They allow you to focus more on pouring your stories onto the digital page. When setting up, pick a theme that reflects the vibe of your travels—something that feels like you. Then, it's all about creating content. Share your first post about a place that struck a chord in your heart or a lesson learned on the road. Remember, your blog is your space; there are no rules. Whether it's daily anecdotes or weekly photo posts, let your content mirror your travel rhythm.

Engaging with your readers is key to growing your blog. Encourage comments, ask questions, and interact with those who take the time to read your stories. This builds a community around your blog and enriches your experience, as you'll find different perspectives enriching your views and memories. Promoting your blog can start with sharing links on your social media platforms or joining blogging communities where like-minded souls gather and share their journeys. The beauty of blogging lies in this connection—the virtual conversations and shared excitement about world explorations.

Blogging also serves as a bridge between you and your family back home. It allows you to share detailed stories and experiences in a more expansive and expressive format than a phone call or text message. Imagine your grandchildren reading about your adventures, seeing your photos, and feeling as if they were right there beside you. It's a wonderful way to maintain a connection with your loved ones, making them feel part of your journeys. Each post can bring them closer to your experiences, helping them understand the world through your eyes.

Moreover, your blog could be a beacon for other seniors contemplating their adventures. Through your posts, you share more than just travel logs; you share inspiration and courage.

Your stories can motivate peers to step out of their comfort zones, pick up their passports, and explore. They see you navigating foreign cities, learning new technologies, and embracing different cultures, and think, "If they can do it, why can't I?" Your blog becomes more than a personal diary; it becomes a rallying cry for active senior living and adventurous spirits.

In wrapping up this chapter on digital storytelling through blogging, we've navigated the essentials of starting a blog, connecting deeply with family and friends, and inspiring a community of like-minded adventurers. Your blog is not just a collection of travel tales but a living, breathing chronicle of your explorations that resonates with and inspires a global audience. As we close this page and look to the next, carry forward the spirit of sharing and connection, ready to explore new horizons in the physical world and the vast, boundless realm of digital storytelling. Let's continue this adventure in the next chapter, where we'll discover more ways to make each travel experience unforgettable.

THIRTEEN

Packing Like a Pro

Imagine you're gearing up for a grand escapade, perhaps a cruise along the Mediterranean or a quaint cabin stay in the Rockies. There's an art to packing, especially when your travel plans stretch across different climates and cultures. It's not just about stuffing a suitcase but curating a capsule of comfort, convenience, and charm. Packing, my dear travelers, is your first step toward a hassle-free holiday. So, let's pack not just clothes but also confidence and a sprinkle of savvy!

Essentials for Every Senior Traveler's Suitcase

Prioritizing Comfort and Necessity

The golden rule of travel for any seasoned adventurer is comfort. Imagine walking the cobbled streets of Santorini or exploring the vast museums of Paris. Now, isn't that more delightful in a pair of well-cushioned shoes that hug your feet like a dear old friend? Yes, shoes can make or break your travel experience, so choosing footwear that offers support and matching various outfits is crucial. Think versatile, think comfort—perhaps a slip-on loafer or a sturdy sandal.

Another key part of smart packing is bringing layered clothing. Weather can be as unpredictable as a market's bargain prices, and layering allows you to adapt without packing three different wardrobes. A breathable base layer, a fleece or sweater, and a waterproof jacket should cover you from the chill of airplane cabins to the breeze of an Alpine morning.

Travel Documentation

In travel, your passport is your golden ticket, travel insurance is your safety net, and knowing whom to call in an emergency is your anchor. Keeping these essentials organized is paramount. A travel document organizer can be a lifesaver, keeping your passport, boarding passes, and insurance details in one neat place. Remember, storing digital backups in a secure cloud service or USB drive is also wise—just in case.

Convenience Items

Let's talk about those little extras that smooth out the wrinkles of travel nuisances. During those delightful but lengthy village tours, a collapsible walking stick can be a knee-saver. Consider this: a portable seat cushion can turn any hard airport bench into a more comfortable waiting spot. Don't forget a lightweight water bottle with a built-in filter to stay hydrated without constantly buying bottled water, which is better for your wallet and the planet.

Safety and Health Gear

No one likes to think about the 'what-ifs' of travel, but a little preparation can go a long way. Packing a basic first-aid kit with band-aids, antiseptic, and your prescribed medications is a must. Hand sanitizer and masks have become as essential as your travel tickets. In today's travel climate, a small pack of disinfectant wipes can keep you feeling secure, whether wiping down a train seat or freshening up after a day of exploration.

Interactive Element: The Ultimate Packing Checklist

Here's an interactive checklist tailored for senior travelers to ensure you've covered all your essentials. Tick each item off as you pack:

- Supportive shoes suitable for multiple occasions
- Layered clothing adaptable to varying climates
- Passport and other essential travel documents
- Digital backups of important documents
- Collapsible walking stick and portable seat cushion
- Lightweight, filter-equipped water bottle
- Basic first-aid kit, including personal medications
- Hand sanitizer, masks, and disinfectant wipes

Packing might seem mundane but think of it as the prelude to your adventure—a ritual that sets the tone for the journey ahead. With each item you place in your suitcase, you're not just packing for a destination; you're preparing for experiences, memories, and the joy of the journey. So, pack smart, pack light, and most importantly, pack with anticipation for the adventures awaiting you.

Gadgets and Gear: Making Travel Comfortable

Ah, the sweet symphony of travel! It's not just about where you go but how comfortably you get there and move around once you've arrived. Let's talk about some tech essentials and comfy gadgets that can transform any trip from good to fabulous, especially tailored for you, the savvy senior traveler. Imagine this: you're all set for your next adventure, and with these handy devices, you'll be cruising through your travels with the ease of a seasoned pro.

Now, let's dive into the world of tech essentials that don't require a tech degree. Smartphones, for instance, are not just phones; they're compact travel offices. Large screens and adjustable fonts help keep your itinerary, boarding passes, and maps at your fingertips. Apps like Google Maps and WhatsApp keep you on track and connected without fuss. Then there's the e-reader, a lightweight library to keep all your favorite books in one place, perfect for in-flight entertainment or a lazy beach day reading. And let's not forget noise-canceling headphones, which can turn a noisy plane cabin into a serene personal listening room, allowing you to enjoy an audiobook or some soothing tunes as you fly.

But what about keeping all these gadgets charged? Ah, the portable charger—a true travel hero — comes into play here. It's like having a power station in your pocket, ensuring your phone, e-reader, or camera is just a plug-in away from being revived. Opt for a model with multiple charges and quick charging capabilities so you're always powered up and ready to go. These tech essentials are designed to be intuitive and user-friendly, ensuring they enhance your travel experience without adding complexity.

Moving on to comfort gadgets, who says you can't have your little bubble of comfort even when you're miles away from home? Let's start with the inflatable neck pillow. Far from the bulky neck pillows of yesteryears, today's versions are compact, inflating in just a few breaths to provide personalized neck support during long flights or train rides. Pair that with compression socks, which keep your feet warm but also help reduce the risk of swelling and deep vein thrombosis (DVT) on longer journeys.

Have you ever been hit with unexpected overweight baggage fees at the airport? An electronic luggage scale is your preemptive solution. This handy gadget lets you weigh your baggage before you leave for the airport, saving you the hassle and expense of repacking in a busy check-in area. These small but mighty devices are easy to use and can be a real game-changer, ensuring you stay within the weight limits with ease.

Let's not overlook the importance of security gadgets. A TSA-approved luggage lock is essential for keeping your belongings secure yet accessible for security checks without damaging your lock or suitcase. Consider also a money belt or a neck pouch, which keeps your money, passport, and other essentials out of sight and close to your body, deterring pickpockets. And when a hotel room feels just a tad too accessible, a portable door lock can add an extra layer of security, giving you peace of mind to enjoy a good night's sleep.

Lastly, the right accessibility tools can make all the difference. For instance, a suitcase with easy-to-maneuver wheels allows you to glide through airports and train stations with minimal effort. And when you need a quick rest, a lightweight folding stool can be invaluable, offering a seat whenever and wherever you need it. Don't forget about a digital magnifier, which is especially handy for reading small print in menus, maps, or timetables, ensuring you remain as independent as ever while navigating new locales.

These gadgets and tools have been thoughtfully designed to add comfort, ease, and a touch of tech-savvy luxury to your travels. They keep you connected, secure, and comfortable, allowing you to focus on making memories and enjoying the experiences rather than sweating the small stuff. So pack these essentials, and you'll be all set to handle whatever adventures come your way with the confidence of a pro traveler.

Toiletries and Medication Checklist

Imagine this: You're all set for your grand adventure, your suitcase packed with just the right outfits, gadgets, and comfort items, but then, halfway through your trip, you realize you've forgotten your blood pressure medication or, perhaps, your favorite skin cream that keeps your skin feeling like it's still in its twenties. Packing medications and toiletries might not be the most exciting part of getting ready for a trip, but it's important. Let's ensure your travel bag is as well-prepared as a Swiss Army knife—equipped for the scenario, leaving no room for those pesky "if only I had packed" moments.

Medication Management

First and foremost, let's tackle the medication problem. Here's a thought—organizing your medications with the precision of a librarian cataloging books will make your travel much smoother. Invest in a good-quality pill organizer that labels each day of the week. This isn't just about keeping your pills in order; it's about peace of mind, knowing you're on track with your health regimen, no matter where in the world you might be. Also, keeping a doctor's note handy for prescription medicines is smart, particularly for international travel, where certain medications might be scrutinized. This document should clearly state your need for the medication, ideally with a note that it's for personal use. It's like having a diplomatic passport for your health needs!

Toiletry Essentials

Moving on to toiletries, let's pack with your skin's needs in mind. As we celebrate more birthdays, our skin asks for more TLC. Opt for hypoallergenic products that promise to be gentle on your skin. This means scouting for soaps, shampoos, and lotions free from common irritants like fragrances and parabens—think of them your skin's best travel buddies. Travel-sized moisturizers are a must, especially with drying conditions aboard flights or in harsher climates than you're used to. And let's not forget the sun protection—a broad-spectrum sunscreen is non-negotiable, whether skiing in the Alps or sunbathing in the Maldives.

Hydration and Nutrition

Now, let's talk hydration and nutrition because exploring on an empty stomach or staying hydrated isn't just about comfort—it's about health. Packing a stash of travel-friendly snacks that cater to any dietary restrictions you might have is a game-changer. Think unsalted nuts, protein bars, or even dried fruits that can give you a quick energy boost without relying on local convenience stores. Also, consider including electrolyte packets in your travel kit. They're lightweight, easy to pack, and can be a lifesaver for replenishing vital salts and minerals, especially after a day of exploring under the sun or recovering from travel-related dehydration.

Personal Hygiene

Lastly, let's ensure your hygiene is nothing less than pristine with a well-thought-out kit. If you use dentures, include cleaning tablets and extra adhesive if necessary. For those managing incontinence, a supply of discreet, travel-friendly products will ensure you can enjoy your travels confidently and comfortably. And pack plenty of antibacterial wipes—they're perfect for freshening up on the go, from sanitizing your hands before a snack to wiping down a seat on public transport. They're the little guardians of cleanliness in your travel arsenal.

Navigating through the maze of toiletries and medications might seem daunting. Still, with these tips, you'll be packing like a pro, equipped for every day of your adventure, ensuring your health, comfort, and hygiene are on par with your excitement for the journey ahead. As you zip up your suitcase, filled with essentials and anticipation of the adventures to come, you're ready to step out the door, confident that you've packed thoughtfully, effectively, and wisely.

As we close this chapter on packing essentials, remember that each item in your suitcase is a building block for a smooth and enjoyable travel experience. From the medication that keeps you healthy to the toiletries that keep you fresh and the snacks that keep you energized—each plays a crucial role in ensuring your travels are as joyful and comfortable as possible. Up next, we'll navigate the exciting world of navigating airports and public transportation, ensuring that your travel logistics are as seamless as your packing strategy. Let the adventures continue with ease and confidence!

FOURTEEN

Navigating Airports and Public Transport

Imagine you're embarking on a grand voyage aboard a majestic airship from a bygone era, navigating through sprawling skyports with adventurers from all corners of the globe. Bring that image back to the 21st century and replace the airship with a modern airplane, but let's keep the excitement alive! Airports can feel like mazes with their endless corridors and myriad gates, but with these savvy tips, you'll be gliding through them with the grace of a seasoned globetrotter. Let's make airport navigation less stressful and more about starting your adventure on the right foot—comfortably and confidently.

Airport Navigation Tips

Early Arrival and Assistance Services

First things first, why rush when you can stroll? Arriving early at the airport is like giving yourself the luxury of time to breathe, explore, and enjoy a coffee while watching planes take off. Aim to arrive a good couple of hours before your flight; this isn't just about catching your breath but also about catching any unforeseen hitches with plenty of time to spare.

Now, airports are champions of assistance services, but here's a little secret: you need to ask for them. Most airports offer dedicated support for seniors, from helping with your luggage to guiding you through the labyrinth of terminals. These services include mobility support, like wheelchairs or motorized carts, and personal escorts through security and to your gate. The trick is to request these services through your airline or the airport's customer service. This way, you're not just a traveler but a VIP with your entourage.

Security Checkpoint Tips

Navigating security doesn't have to feel like unraveling a Rubik's cube. The key here is simplicity. Wear shoes that you can slip off easily—think loafers or slip-ons—since you might need to remove them during security checks. Keep your liquids (including gels and aerosols) in a clear, resealable plastic bag and under the limit of 3.4 ounces (100 milliliters). Lay them out in the tray, not buried in your carry-on, to keep things moving smoothly.

Familiarize yourself with TSA's senior-specific allowances, such as being able to stay seated during checks if standing is a challenge or requesting a hand-check of medications and sensitive devices like pacemakers. Don't hesitate to communicate your needs to the security officers—they're there to help make your transit as smooth as possible.

Relaxation and Waiting Areas

Airports are not just non-stop hubs; they also have their quiet corners and oases of comfort. Many airports feature designated relaxation areas where you can escape the hustle and bustle. These spots often have more comfortable seating, reduced noise, and sometimes even soothing visuals like aquariums or gardens.

Check if your credit card grants you access to airport lounges for a touch of luxury. These lounges aren't just about plush sofas and free snacks; they offer a quieter environment to relax or even take a quick nap. Some lounges also provide additional services like showers and private workspaces, turning your waiting time into a mini-retreat.

Boarding and In-flight Comfort

When it comes to boarding, remember that seniors are often entitled to priority boarding. Take advantage of this to settle on the plane without the pressure of queues nudging at your back. Choose your seat wisely—aisle seats near the front can give you more legroom and easier access when boarding and disembarking.

Onboard comfort is about little luxuries. Bring a neck pillow, a light blanket, and a good book or an e-reader loaded with your favorite novels. Stay hydrated throughout the flight—airplane cabins are notoriously dry. Most importantly, keep any medications you need during the flight in your carry-on, not stowed above in the overhead bins. This way, you're prepared for a comfortable flight, soaring above the clouds in a plane and spirits.

Interactive Element: Airport Comfort Checklist

Before you head to the airport, run through this quick checklist to ensure a smooth and comfortable airport experience:

- Confirm assistance services with your airline at least 48 hours before departure.
- Pack liquids in a clear, accessible bag for easy security screening.
- Choose comfortable, easy-to-remove footwear.
- Check if your credit card provides access to airport lounges.
- Opt for priority boarding to ease your boarding process.
- Prepare a small comfort kit for in-flight use, including hydration aids, a neck pillow, and entertainment options.

Navigating airports with these tips turns a potentially hectic part of your travel into an enjoyable prelude to your adventure. With some planning and the right mindset, every step through the airport can be taken easily and confidently, setting a joyful tone for the wonderful experiences that await you at your destination.

Mastering Public Transportation Abroad

Navigating public transportation in a new city can feel like solving a crossword puzzle — it starts perplexing, but once you get the hang of it, there's a sense of accomplishment in every correct move. Whether it's the bustling metros of Paris or the iconic trams of San Francisco, each system has its quirks and charms. Before you pack your suitcase, homework on your destination's public transport options can save you time, money, and stress. Websites and apps are your best friends here, providing real-time data on bus schedules, metro lines, and even which car to board for the best exit at your stop. Google Maps, Citymapper, and Moovit are like having digital travel guides in your pocket. They give you step-by-step directions and updates, making public transport easy to navigate and more like a fun local adventure.

Isn't it wonderful to flash a card and breeze through like a local? Many cities offer public transportation discounts for seniors, but these gems aren't always advertised. The perks vary widely from reduced fare cards to free travel passes, so it's worth investigating before you go. Often, you might need to apply for these discounts in advance or show some ID to qualify, but the effort can halve your travel costs. For example, in London, the Freedom Pass allows seniors over a certain age to travel free on buses, tubes, and other forms of public transport, which is economical and encourages you to hop on and explore easily.

Regarding etiquette and safety on public transport, a few savvy tips can ensure your ride is smooth and secure. Always keep your belongings close — a crossbody bag or a fanny pack worn to the front is less likely to be tampered with than a backpack. Be aware of peak hours, which can be overwhelming; traveling during off-peak times can offer a more relaxed journey. Every place has its unspoken rules, whether standing on the right side of the escalator in London or avoiding eye contact in Tokyo subways. Observing locals can provide valuable cues on how to blend in and use the public systems respectfully and efficiently.

The world has become more accessible, but physical accessibility varies greatly from one country to another. Thankfully, many major cities are improving access to public transportation for travelers with mobility issues. Features like low-floor buses and trains with dedicated spaces for wheelchairs and stations equipped with elevators and tactile paths are becoming more common. Before you travel, check out the transit authority's website for accessibility features or contact them directly with your questions. Some cities even offer accessibility maps or guides that can help you confidently plan your routes, ensuring that your travel is possible and enjoyable.

Navigating public transport abroad doesn't have to be a daunting endeavor. With a mix of prior research, utilizing the right apps, taking advantage of senior discounts, and following local customs, you can master the local transit system and discover the joys of moving around the city like someone who's been doing it for years. So, embrace these tools and tips, and you'll not just travel in these cities — you'll traverse them with the ease and savvy of a local, making your trip all the richer and more rewarding.

Renting a Car Abroad

Ah, the freedom of the open road! There's something undeniably thrilling about zipping along a coastal highway or winding through quaint village streets in a car that's yours (temporarily, of course). Renting a car while traveling abroad adds a layer of convenience to your voyage and offers the liberty to explore at your own pace, stopping where and when you want. Before you hit the road, doing some planning can make sure your trip is more about enjoying the scenery and less about dealing with logistics.

When picking the perfect rental car, consider what you need for a comfortable ride. Automatic transmissions are your friend here, particularly if you're used to driving one back home. Why wrestle with a manual shifter while also navigating unfamiliar roads? Also, consider the size of the vehicle. While a larger car may offer more comfort and space, a compact model can be easier to handle, especially in cities with narrow lanes or limited parking. Most rental companies offer a range of options, so you can choose one that feels like a good fit for your driving skills and travel needs.

Now, let's talk about the tech side: using GPS. This little gadget can be a lifesaver, turning a potentially wrong turn into a simple, stress-free journey. Many rental cars come equipped with GPS, but it's always a good idea to confirm this when you book. Alternatively, consider using your smartphone's GPS capabilities, which can be just as effective, provided you can access local data or download maps for offline use. Either way, having a reliable navigator on hand can make all the difference, letting you focus on the journey and the stunning views rather than squinting at confusing road signs.

Navigating local driving laws and requirements is next on your checklist. Every country has its own driving rules, and some might surprise you. For instance, did you know that turning right on red is illegal in some places? Or that there are specific lanes you must use in others if you're driving slower than other traffic? Before you start your engine, take some time to familiarize yourself with these rules. It's also wise to check if you need an International Driving Permit (IDP) and your regular driver's license. These permits can usually be obtained easily in your home country and can be invaluable for driving legally abroad.

Insurance is another crucial element to consider. While it might be tempting to skip the extra expense, the right insurance coverage can provide priceless peace of mind. Opt for a plan that covers not just collisions but also theft and personal injury, especially in places where you might be liable for hefty damages. Check if your credit card offers any coverage for car rentals—many do, and this can sometimes be sufficient. However, ensure you understand what's covered and what's not. It's all about balancing cost against risk—spending more on comprehensive coverage could save you a fortune in an unlikely accident.

Lastly, let's talk about preparing for emergencies. No one likes to think about them, but being prepared can drastically improve the outcomes of unexpected situations. Always have a basic road safety kit in your car, including a first-aid kit, a flashlight, and reflective warning signs. Ensure your mobile phone is always charged when you set off on longer trips, and consider carrying a portable charger. Familiarize yourself with local emergency numbers and keep them handy. Additionally, renting a car with a local SIM card can be smart, ensuring you can make calls or access data without excessive roaming charges.

Navigating car rentals and driving abroad doesn't have to be daunting. With the right preparation, you can enjoy the freedom and flexibility of exploring new destinations at your own pace, with the wind in your hair and a road map in the glove compartment. Remember to take it slow, soak in the sights, and drive safely. Let's gear up for the next chapter, where we'll uncover more insights to enhance your travel experiences, ensuring each adventure is as fulfilling and hassle-free as possible.

FIFTEEN

Budget-Friendly Travel Hacks

Imagine you're a treasure hunter, not scouring sandy beaches with a metal detector but navigating the bustling digital marketplace for the shiniest travel deals. Each discount, each special offer you unearth, is a golden coin added to your vacation vault. It's a thrilling quest, isn't it? Scoring the best travel deals isn't just about saving a few bucks—it's about smartly extending your travel budget to pack more adventure, more experiences, and perhaps a few extra souvenirs into your journey. So, let's dive into some savvy strategies that will have you booking like a pro, ensuring your golden years are filled with golden travel opportunities without breaking the bank.

Finding the Best Deals on Flights and Accommodations

Timing and Flexibility

What is the secret sauce to snagging fabulous flight and accommodation deals? Timing and flexibility. Picture this:

while most travelers are locked into peak holiday seasons and rigid travel dates, you, the astute traveler, can play the field. Flying mid-week or during shoulder seasons (those magical times right before or after peak tourist seasons) can dramatically decrease costs. Airlines and hotels are eager to fill seats and rooms that might otherwise remain empty.

For instance, consider visiting Europe in the fall instead of summer. You'll enjoy mild weather, fewer crowds, and significantly lower prices. Flexibility in your destination can also lead to unexpected savings. Have you ever considered swapping the beaches of Maui for the less-trodden sands of the Azores? Such swaps can lead to discovering incredible locations at a fraction of the price. Embrace the offbeat and unexpected; sometimes, the road less traveled is less expensive, too!

Comparison and Alerts

Harness the power of technology to become a real detective. Use comparison websites like Kayak, Skyscanner, or Google Flights to compare prices across numerous airlines and booking sites. But don't just stop there—turn on price alerts for your desired routes. These handy notifications mean you don't need to check prices obsessively. Instead, you'll receive an alert when prices drop, allowing you to book when the cost hits your target price. It's like having a personal assistant dedicated to catching deals!

Loyalty Programs

Loyalty, in the travel world, definitely has its perks. Enrolling in airline and hotel loyalty programs often costs nothing but can yield substantial rewards. Accumulate points or miles with your favorite travel brands or a co-branded credit card. Over time, these points can be redeemed for free flights, hotel stays, upgrades, and even luxurious perks like airport lounge access—imagine relaxing in a plush lounge, cocktail in hand, rather than perching on a hard airport gate seat!

Alternative Accommodations

Hotels are just one piece of the accommodation puzzle. Have you considered a charming bed and breakfast or a stylish vacation rental? Platforms like Airbnb or Vrbo often offer more bang for your buck and provide a richer, more authentic stay. Imagine renting a quaint cottage in Tuscany or a chic apartment in the heart of New Orleans. Plus, these accommodations typically offer kitchens, which means you can save further by preparing some meals at home—a win for both your budget and your taste buds!

Interactive Element: Accommodation Comparison Exercise

To truly grasp the benefits of alternative accommodations, why not try a little comparison exercise? Next time you plan a trip, compare the cost of a week-long hotel stay with a week at a vacation rental in the same area—factor in additional savings from having access to a kitchen and other amenities like free parking or laundry. You might be surprised at how much cheaper (and nicer!) the alternative can be.

Travel hacking isn't just about being frugal; it's about being resourceful and open to new experiences that save money and enhance your travel adventures. With these strategies, you're saving money and paving the way for more travel, discovery, and memorable moments. So, keep these tips in your travel toolkit, and you're sure to master the art of budget-friendly travel, making each trip not just a journey but a smart adventure.

Enjoying Luxury Experiences on a Budget

Who says luxury and budget can't go hand in hand? Ah, the sweet joy of indulging in the finer things while keeping your wallet happy—it's almost like having your cake and eating it, too! Let's unravel some clever ways to add a touch of luxury to your travels without the opulent price tag. It's all about knowing when to travel, where to look for the best deals, and how to access those plush experiences without splurging.

Off-Peak Travel

Imagine having a luxurious beach resort almost all to yourself, where the only footprints in the sand are yours, or attending a world-class opera with seats so good you can see the conductor's every expression. This isn't just a daydream; it can be your reality if you travel during off-peak times. When the crowds thin out, many high-end resorts and cultural venues drop prices to attract more visitors. Traveling during these quieter times saves you money and enhances your experience—fewer people mean more personalized service and an unhurried, uncrowded atmosphere. Picture enjoying a sunset from a prime spot on the balcony of a five-star hotel or getting a spa appointment with all the extras because there's an off-season discount and fewer guests to accommodate!

Group Tours and Packages

Let's talk about the magic of group tours and package deals. Operators often negotiate rates much lower than you could get booking because they're bringing in volume. And no, we're not talking about those tours where you're herded around with a flag-waving guide. Today's luxury group tours are about small, exclusive experiences with perks, including private viewings of museums, dinners prepared by top chefs, or visits to private vineyards. These packages can offer you the crème de la crème of travel experiences at a fraction of the cost. You could be sipping champagne on a private balcony overlooking the French Riviera or enjoying a gourmet meal after a private tour of an ancient castle, all arranged by your tour operator at a more palatable package price.

Last-Minute Deals

For spontaneous travelers, last-minute deals can be the ticket to luxury. Many high-end resorts, cruise lines, and boutique hotels offer significant discounts to fill rooms and spaces at the eleventh hour. These can often be found on luxury travel websites or through direct newsletters from the resorts. Imagine booking a cruise suite at half the price or snagging a stay at a boutique hotel for less than a standard room simply because you could book a week before departure. It's like the travel gods are rewarding you for your willingness to embrace spontaneity!

Cultural Passes

Lastly, let's not underestimate the value of a good city cultural pass. These passes, often available for a single purchase, can open doors to a city's top museums, galleries, and sometimes even concerts and performances. They come with the added benefit of skipping the long lines, which feels like a luxury. Whether it's the New York CityPASS or the Paris Museum Pass, you get more than entry tickets. You're getting a pass to explore the city's cultural highlights at your own pace. It's affordable, convenient, and lets you enjoy the culture without breaking the bank.

Navigating the landscape of luxury travel doesn't require a treasure map; it just needs a bit of savvy planning, a dash of flexibility, and an appetite for life's finer experiences. With these strategies, you can elevate your travel experiences, peppering your trips with luxury without the lavish expense. So go ahead and add a little luxury to your adventures—you've earned it, and with these hacks, you certainly can afford it!

Free and Low-Cost Attractions Worth Visiting

Who says you need to spend a fortune to enjoy the richness of travel? Let's peel back the curtain on the world of free and low-cost attractions that promise to enrich your travel diary without thinning your wallet. Picture this: you are reveling in the beauty of lush gardens, soaking up history in grand museums, and strolling through vibrant markets—all without spending a dime. It's like finding hidden treasures in plain sight, and who doesn't enjoy a good treasure hunt?

Public Spaces and Nature

Imagine stepping into a sprawling park in the heart of a bustling city, where the only skyscrapers are towering trees, and the symphony of chirping birds replaces the sounds of traffic. Public spaces such as parks, gardens, and natural reserves are not just spots to catch a breath; they are gateways to experiencing a city's soul. Many of these green spaces are free to visit, providing a peaceful escape in the middle of the city. Take, for example, the iconic Central Park in New York or the Royal Botanic Gardens in Melbourne. Both provide a canvas of natural beauty, perfect for strolls or impromptu picnics. These spaces often hold the key to understanding a city's layout and people's way of life, offering scenic views and a peek into everyday local interactions.

Beyond the greenery, public spaces often serve as cultural showcases. From awe-inspiring public art installations in Chicago's Millennium Park to historical landmarks dotted around Rome's public plazas, the fusion of nature, architecture, and art offers a multi-sensory experience that doesn't cost a penny. These areas are perfect for those leisurely days when you have no set itinerary but a simple desire to explore and absorb.

Community Events and Markets

Now, let's turn the pages to the vibrant community events and markets, where the entry price is often free, but the experience is priceless. Local markets and community festivals offer a kaleidoscope of local traditions, crafts, and foods, providing a grassroots feel of the destination's cultural heartbeat. Imagine wandering through the bustling night markets in Taipei or celebrating the festive spirit at Munich's Christmas markets. These are places where you can taste local delicacies, chat with artisans, and witness the communal spirit that defines a locality.

Moreover, community events such as local music festivals, street performances, and art fairs entertain and provide a chance to mingle with locals and travelers, creating a sense of global community. Whether listening to jazz on the streets of New Orleans or watching a traditional dance performance in Bali, these experiences add layers of understanding and enjoyment to your travels that luxury tours seldom provide.

Museum Free Days

For the culturally curious, museums can be treasure troves of knowledge and beauty, and guess what? Many world-renowned museums offer days when admission is free. This open-door policy allows you to gaze upon masterpieces without the masterpiece of a price tag. Institutions like the Louvre in Paris and the Smithsonian museums in Washington, D.C., open their doors for free on certain days, inviting everyone to explore vast collections of art, history, and science.

These free days are perfect for delving into new subjects or spending extra time with your favorite exhibits without the pressure of getting your money's worth. It's like having a backstage pass to the corridors of history and creativity, where every visit can offer new insights and inspirations.

Walking and Audio Tours

Lastly, let's lace up our walking shoes for guided explorations that won't drain your wallet. Many cities offer free or low-cost walking tours led by locals passionate about sharing their knowledge and love for their city. These tours can take you through historic neighborhoods, significant landmarks, or themed routes like ghost tours or culinary trails. For a more personal pace, downloadable audio tours can provide a rich narrative to your self-guided walks, available with a few taps on your smartphone.

These walking adventures are not just about physical activity; they're about stitching together the fabric of a city's story as you move through it. They allow you to pause, observe, and interact in ways that bus tours or hurried sightseeing can't match, offering a deeper connection to the places you visit.

As we wrap up this treasure trove of budget-friendly travel gems, remember that the value of these experiences lies not in their price but in their ability to enrich your travels with authentic insights and joyous moments. Next, we'll navigate the exciting possibilities of building a community of fellow travelers, where sharing experiences and tips can make every journey even more rewarding. Keep your map handy—we're continuing this adventure together, exploring further and deeper, yet always mindful of the joys that cost little but bring immense happiness.

SIXTEEN

Building a Community of Senior Travelers

Imagine stepping into a grand ballroom where everyone's dance steps match your rhythm, and the music echoes your favorite tunes. That's the harmony and connection in travel groups and clubs tailored to seniors. It's not just about having company; it's about sharing the journey with people who tap their feet to the same beat of adventure as you do. So, let's chat about why finding your tribe can turn travel into a more enriching and secure experience, especially as you explore the golden years of your life.

Joining Travel Groups and Clubs for Seniors

Finding Your Tribe

When you join a travel group or club that caters to seniors, you're not just adding destinations to your itinerary; you're enriching your travel experience with companionship and shared insights. These groups often become more than travel buddies; they become a community where stories, tips, and laughter are shared freely. Imagine the comfort of having a friend who remembers the same TV shows and music hits from back in the day, discussing these over a cup of coffee in a Parisian café or while watching a sunset in Santorini.

Travel clubs and groups also open up a world of opportunities that might be daunting to tackle solo. They can offer exclusive deals, organized tours, and activities tailored to seniors. These include leisurely-paced cultural tours, cruises with special accommodations, or adventure activities that respect your comfort and physical limits. The collective knowledge and experiences of the group can make travel smoother and, often, more affordable.

Types of Groups

The variety of senior travel groups is as diverse as the places they visit. You might find groups focusing on luxury travel, offering stays in high-end accommodations and gourmet dining experiences. Other groups might lean toward adventure, organizing hikes, cycling tours, or wildlife safaris. Then, cultural immersion groups aim to explore the traditions and histories of the destinations deeply.

Social media-based communities are particularly accessible and can connect you with fellow senior travelers worldwide. Platforms like Facebook have numerous senior travel groups where members share advice, post travel photos, and even arrange meetups. On the other hand, local clubs often meet in person regularly, discuss travel plans, share presentations, and organize local outings to keep the spirit of travel alive between bigger trips.

Engagement and Participation

Active participation in these groups can significantly enhance your sense of belonging and community. Attending meetings and social events, joining group trips, and volunteering to help organize events can make you feel more connected and invested in the group. Such engagement also fosters a sense of purpose and contribution, which is immensely fulfilling.

Consider hosting a pre-trip planning session or a post-trip photo-sharing meetup. These gatherings can be fun and informative, helping to build excitement and camaraderie among members. They also provide a platform to share your skills and knowledge, perhaps in photography, blogging, or a particular language.

Safety in Numbers

Traveling with a group inherently boosts your sense of security. There's safety in numbers, whether you're navigating the crowded streets of a bustling city or exploring remote areas. Group leaders often handle unexpected challenges more efficiently, thanks to their experience and the collective resources of the group. For anyone apprehensive about solo travel, these groups provide a comforting assurance that you're not alone, that there are people who have your back, ready to help or share a good laugh over a missed train or a funny travel mishap.

Interactive Element: Group Travel Engagement Quiz

To find out how you can best engage in a senior travel group, here's a quick quiz to match your interests with group activities:

- **What type of travel most interests you?** (A) Cultural immersion (B) Adventure (C) Relaxation
- **What role do you enjoy in group settings?** (A) Organizer (B) Participant (C) Observer
- **What's your preferred group size?** (A) Small, intimate groups (B) Large, diverse groups
- **How active do you like your travels?** (A) Very active, lots of walking/hiking (B) Moderately active, balanced activities (C) Low-key, more relaxed tours

Your answers can guide you to the type of senior travel group and the role you might enjoy most, ensuring every trip is not just a journey but a joyous gathering of like-minded souls. So, as you consider your next travel plans, consider joining a senior travel group—it might just be the key to unlocking a more fulfilling, secure, and enjoyable travel experience.

Sharing Your Travel Experiences

Ah, the joy of returning from a trip with a suitcase bulging not just with souvenirs but stories, each a sparkling gem just waiting to be shared. Imagine gathering a crowd, drawing them in with tales of distant lands, unexpected adventures, and personal revelations. Sharing your travel experiences isn't just about recounting where you went and what you saw; it's about transporting your audience right there with you through the power of your words and images. Let's explore how you can turn your travel stories into captivating tales that entertain, inspire, and connect with your listeners.

Crafting Your Story

Writing a great travel story is like creating art. Start by sharing your experiences with vivid details, emotions, and how the journey helped you grow. Think about that sunset that painted the sky in hues of gold and purple in Santorini or the spicy aroma of street food in Bangkok that made your mouth water. These aren't just details; they're the essence of your story, bringing it to life. But here's the secret ingredient: personal growth. Share not just what changed around you but what changed within you. Maybe navigating the maze-like streets of Venice taught you patience, or meeting locals in a remote village in Peru showed you new perspectives on happiness. These revelations make your story resonate on a deeper level, giving your audience a glimpse into the transformative power of travel.

When structuring your story, think of it as a journey—there's a beginning, where you set the scene, introduce the characters, and hint at the adventures to come. The middle is your playground, full of challenges, highlights, and the heart of your narrative. And finally, the end, where you tie it all together, reflecting on the lessons learned and the memories made. This structure doesn't just keep your content organized; it ensures your audience stays with you, eager to hear what happens next.

Presentation Skills

A great story needs a great storyteller. Developing your presentation skills can turn a good story into an unforgettable experience. Start with your visuals; they're your backdrop, setting the scene. Create photo slideshows or videos that complement your narrative, choosing images that evoke emotion or illustrate your tales. Tools like PowerPoint or Canva can help you design engaging presentations with ease.

Now, let's talk delivery. How you share your story can be as impactful as the story itself. Practice your pacing, your tone, and your body language. Keep your style conversational and inviting, as if you're sharing a coffee with friends, not lecturing in a classroom. And here's a little trick: use pauses. A well-timed pause can allow your audience to absorb a poignant point or laugh with you at a humorous anecdote.

Finding Venues

Finding the right venue to share your stories can amplify their impact. Local community centers, libraries, and travel clubs often welcome guest speakers and provide a ready audience that shares your interest in travel. These places usually have the facilities you need, like projectors and seating, and they can help promote your talk to their members.

Don't overlook online platforms, especially if mobility or distance is a constraint. Webinars, live Zoom, or Facebook Live sessions can reach a broader audience. You might be speaking from your living room, but your story can touch people across the globe. These platforms often allow for interactive elements like Q&A sessions, making your presentation a two-way conversation that engages and connects.

Feedback and Improvement

Lastly, embrace feedback. Every talk you give is a stepping stone to becoming a better storyteller. Encourage your audience to share their thoughts and suggestions. What did they love? What didn't resonate as much? This feedback is invaluable, helping you refine your skills and better connect with your listeners in future presentations. Remember, each talk is not just a performance; it's a conversation, an exchange of experiences and perspectives that enriches you and your audience.

By sharing your travel experiences, you're doing more than recounting tales; you're inviting others to see the world through your eyes, inspiring them to embark on their adventures. So, take these tips, craft your story, and step into the spotlight. The stage is yours, and your audience awaits.

Planning Your Next Adventure

Ah, the thrill of plotting a new adventure—it's like sketching out a dream on the canvas of your calendar. But here's the thing: staying inspired and connected between trips is just as crucial as the trips themselves. It keeps the travel flame alive, flickering with possibilities and anticipation. Let's dive into how continuous learning, goal setting, and staying connected can transform how you view and plan your travels, turning each adventure into a chapter of an ever-expanding epic.

Continuous Learning

Think of yourself as a student with the world as your classroom. There's always something new to learn—a hidden cultural nuance of a remote village or the latest travel gadget that could change the way you trek. Dive into travel documentaries showing exotic lands while lounging in your living room. Each documentary can open new avenues of exploration and add layers of understanding to places you thought you knew.

Books about travel or set in distant locales can also stoke your wanderlust. Imagine reading about the lavender fields of Provence in winter and then walking through them come summer, the fragrant blooms buzzing with life, just as you imagined—or even better. Blogs offer a more personal touch, with advice and stories from fellow travelers who've been where you dream to go. They can offer the nitty-gritty details that documentaries and books might gloss over, from the best street food stalls to tips for navigating local transit.

Setting Travel Goals

Now, about those dreams sketched on your calendar—turning them into concrete goals can make all the difference. Reflect on your past travels. What experiences made you feel most alive? Was it the tranquility of rural landscapes or the bustling energy of urban centers? Use these reflections to shape your travel goals. Maybe it's time to tick off those bucket-list destinations you've been eyeing for years or to challenge yourself with adventures a bit out of your comfort zone, like a safari in the Serengeti or a culinary tour through India.

Setting specific travel themes can also add an exciting twist to your adventures. Perhaps you'd like to spend a year exploring ancient ruins or a season discovering the world's best beaches. These themes can guide your research and planning, making the process as exhilarating as the travel itself. And remember, each trip builds your confidence and capability, pushing your boundaries and expanding your horizons.

Staying Connected

Engaging with the vast and vibrant travel community can unexpectedly enrich your life. Social media platforms are bustling hubs where ideas and inspirations flourish. Follow travel influencers whose style you admire, join Facebook groups focused on senior travel, or engage in Instagram's travel community. These platforms provide travel inspiration, practical advice, and a chance to interact with fellow travelers who share your passions and curiosities.

Don't underestimate the joy of regular meetups with local travel clubs or attending travel-themed events where you can mingle with like-minded adventurers. These gatherings can be a treasure trove of information and provide a sense of community that sustains your travel spirit. Online forums and travel blogs are also splendid places to ask questions, share experiences, and keep your finger on the pulse of the travel world.

Preparation and Anticipation

Let's not forget the sweet anticipation of preparing for a trip. It's a part of the adventure itself. Delving into research, booking your next getaway, and even daydreaming about it can be incredibly joyful and fulfilling. This phase is your playground—draft itineraries, check out maps, learn a few phrases in the language of your next destination, or start packing. Each step brings you closer to your next great adventure, building excitement and anticipation.

This preparatory phase is also a perfect time for reflection. Consider what you've learned from previous trips and how you can apply those insights to enhance your next experience. Maybe it's deciding to pack lighter, leave more room for spontaneity, or stay longer in a place to soak in its essence. Whatever your conclusions, let them guide you to smarter, more enjoyable travels.

In wrapping up this chapter, remember that a traveler's journey never pauses; it only takes different forms. Whether you're learning from documentaries, setting audacious travel goals, staying connected with the global travel community, or savoring the anticipation of your next adventure, you're continuously on a path of discovery. So keep your maps handy and your curiosity alive, for every day brings a new opportunity to explore, learn, and connect.

As we close this chapter on staying inspired and connected, we turn the page to exploring how travel impacts us deeply, not just during the journey but long after we've returned home. Stay tuned as we delve into the transformative power of travel and how it reshapes our perspectives and enriches our lives.

Conclusion

Well, here we are at the end of a fantastic journey together, not just through the pages of this book but through the endless possibilities that travel holds for each of us in our golden years. As we've explored together, traveling isn't just about ticking destinations off a list; it's a profound avenue for personal growth, brimming with opportunities for learning, laughter, and the kind of liberty that only comes when packing a suitcase and stepping into a new adventure.

From navigating the ever-evolving digital world to planning trips that resonate with our deepest desires, this book aims to arm you with everything you need to turn the dream of travel into a delightful reality. We've delved into how embracing solo and group travel can open doors to new friendships, experiences, and insights, irrespective of age. Remember, each trip is a brushstroke in the beautiful painting of your life.

We've underscored the importance of staying curious and engaged through learning and volunteering, enriching your travels and, indeed, your life. Each destination, from the cobblestone streets of Europe to the vibrant markets of Southeast Asia, offers a unique classroom experience. And let's remember the joy of documenting these moments. Whether through photographs, journals, or blogs, capturing your travel tales preserves memories and shares the spark of adventure with others.

As you flip each page and plan your journeys, I encourage you to wield the power of technology, not as a challenge but as a trusty travel companion that opens up new horizons with just a few taps. Stay open to new experiences, whether trying out a local dance or sampling exotic cuisine and let these moments transform you.

I urge you, my fellow wanderers, to not just dream about places you wish to see but to take definitive steps toward experiencing them. Whether it's the serene landscapes of New Zealand or the historic wonders of Egypt, every corner of the world offers something extraordinary that you are just waiting to discover.

Build and nurture the community of senior travelers. Share your stories and tips, and revel in such a community's collective wisdom and support. Together, we can redefine what it means to travel in our senior years, turning every journey into a shared celebration.

In closing, I hope this book serves as a guide and a launchpad for your adventures. May it inspire you to step out with confidence, curiosity, and a bit of that adventurous spirit that makes life so thrilling. Remember, exploring new horizons and creating new memories is always possible. The world is vast, vibrant, and inviting—so pack your bags, embrace the journey, and let every mile enrich your golden years.

Safe travels, dear friends. May each journey bring joy, enlightenment, and many stories and photo albums to fill your heart. Here's to our travels—may they be as endless as they are enriching!

Keeping the Adventure Alive

Now that you have everything you need to embark on stress-free, enriching travels, it's time to share your new-found knowledge and help other readers discover the same joy.

Leaving your honest opinion of this book on Amazon will show other senior travelers where they can find the guidance they need to enjoy their own adventures.

Thank you for your help. Travel is kept alive when we share our experiences, and you're helping me to do just that.

Simply scan the QR code below to leave your review:

Let's keep the adventure alive, passing on the joy of travel and inspiring others to explore the world. Your role in this journey is crucial, and I am deeply grateful for your help in making senior travel accessible and exciting for all.

Here's to continuing our exploration, armed with new knowledge and a shared purpose. Thank you for being an essential part of this journey.

Your biggest fan,

Pauline Winslow

References

- *DESTINATION AGING: The Health Benefits of Travel* https://friendshipcenters.org/destination-aging-the-health-benefits-of-travel/
- *Best Tips to Help With Travel Anxiety* https://www.roadscholar.org/blog/tips-to-help-with-traveling-anxiety/
- *What is Slow Travel, and What are the Benefits?* https://www.notintheguidebooks.com/sustainability/what-is-slow-travel-and-what-are-the-benefits/
- *How This 70 Year Old Couple Traveled the World* https://www.nomadicmatt.com/travel-blogs/don-alison-success-story/
- *8 Great Travel Apps for Seniors* https://www.torrancememorial.org/healthy-living/blog/8-great-travel-apps-for-seniors/
- *Traveling Securely: A Comprehensive Guide to Protecting Your Digital Footprint While on the Move* https://staysafeonline.org/resources/traveling-securely-a-comprehensive-guide-to-protecting-your-digital-footprint-while-on-the-move/
- *14 Best Senior Travel Groups That Offer All Kinds of Adventures!* https://community.aarp.org/t5/Destinations/%EF%B8%8F-14-Best-Senior-Travel-Groups-That-Offer-All-Kinds-of/m-p/2501720
- *The Senior's Guide to Online Safety* https://connectsafely.org/seniors-guide-to-online-safety/
- *Best (And Worst) Destinations For Senior Travel According ...* https://www.forbes.com/sites/lealane/2023/06/30/best-and-worst-destinations-for-senior-travel-according-to-new-data/
- *Senior Travel Insurance: What to Know* https://www.nerdwallet.com/article/travel/senior-travel-insurance
- *Thrifty Strategies for Senior Travelers* https://www.nytimes.com/2022/09/22/travel/frugal-strategies-for-senior-travelers.html
- *45 Senior Travel Discounts* https://www.aarp.org/money/budgeting-saving/info-2017/senior-travel-discounts-fd.html
- *Travel Solo Over 60: Mature, Strong and Confident* https://solotravelerworld.com/travel-solo-over-60-strong-confident/
- *10 Best Senior Travel Tour Companies & Reviews | 2024/2025* https://www.travelstride.com/tc/senior-travel-tour-companies

- *Loneliness and Social Isolation — Tips for Staying Connected* https://www.nia.nih.gov/health/loneliness-and-social-isolation/loneliness-and-social-isolation-tips-staying-connected
- *Safe Travel Tips for Older Adults* https://ncoa.org/article/safe-travel-tips-for-older-adults
- *Older Adults and Healthy Travel - CDC* https://wwwnc.cdc.gov/travel/page/senior-citizens
- *Exercise Plan for Seniors: Strength, Stretching, and Balance* https://www.healthline.com/health/everyday-fitness/senior-workouts
- *6 Tips for Managing Dietary Restrictions While Abroad* https://www.diversityabroad.com/articles/6-tips-managing-dietary-restrictions-while-abroad
- *The Best Senior Travel Insurance Companies of 2024* https://www.marketwatch.com/guides/insurance-services/senior-travel-insurance/
- *Educational Small Group Culinary Tours for Senior Citizens* https://www.roadscholar.org/collections/food--wine/
- *Essential Bird Watching Equipment for Seniors* https://seniorslifestylemag.com/health-well-being/essential-bird-watching-equipment-for-seniors/
- *Arts for the Aging | Artistic expression when words fail* https://artsfortheaging.org/
- *Senior Festival Tours - Programs For Festival Lovers* https://www.roadscholar.org/browse-collections/festivals/
- *5 of the Most Accessible Destinations in Eastern Europe* https://www.handiscover.com/fr-fr/content/post/accessible-destinations-in-eastern-europe--en
- *Advice for Seniors for Safe Travel in Asia* https://www.xyzasia.com/home/advice-for-seniors-for-safe-travel-in-asia
- *Icons of Costa Rica Eco Tour for Seniors* https://www.zicasso.com/i/costa-rica/icons-costa-rica-eco-tour-seniors
- *Travel Tips for Seniors to Prevent Illnesses While on Vacation* https://www.seniorhelpers.com/ct/danbury/resources/news-and-blog/travel-tips-for-seniors-to-prevent-illnesses-while-on-vacation/
- *7 of the Best National Parks for Seniors* https://www.travelandleisure.com/best-national-parks-for-seniors-6735739
- *The 10 Best Beach Towns to Retire in the U.S.* https://money.usnews.com/money/retirement/articles/the-10-best-beach-towns-to-retire-in-the-u-s

- *Accessibility for Visitors* https://www.si.edu/visit/accessibility
- *Best Historical Cities to Visit in the USA - U.S. News Travel* https://travel.usnews.com/rankings/best-us-historic-destinations/
- *The most accessible cities in Europe for 2024* https://www.cntraveller.com/article/most-accessible-cities-europe
- *Australia and New Zealand Tours For Seniors* https://www.roadscholar.org/collections/australia-new-zealand/
- *Discovering 5 Senior-Friendly Destinations in Asia and ...* https://www.klook.com/en-PH/blog/senior-friendly-destinations-asia-europe/
- *The Seoul 50+ initiative in South Korea* https://www.centreforpublicimpact.org/case-study/seoul-50plus
- *Walking Tours | Small Group Experiences for Seniors* https://www.odysseytraveller.com/tour-category/hiking-walking/
- *Top 5 Yoga Retreats for Seniors* https://www.healthandfitnesstravel.com/blog/top-5-yoga-retreats-for-seniors
- *Senior & Active Adult Cycling Adventure Tours* https://seniorcycling.com/
- *DESTINATION AGING: The Health Benefits of Travel* https://friendshipcenters.org/destination-aging-the-health-benefits-of-travel/
- *Language Immersion Programs for Seniors: Never Too Old ...* https://www.goabroad.com/articles/language-study-abroad/language-immersion-programs-for-seniors
- *Volunteer Abroad Opportunities for Seniors and Retirees* https://www.volunteerforever.com/article_post/volunteer-abroad-opportunities-for-seniors-and-retirees/
- *Top 10 Best and Most Tempting Cooking School Vacations for Seniors* https://www.cooking-vacations.com/842/top-10-best-and-most-tempting-cooking-school-vacations-for-seniors/
- *How to Plan a Memorable Wine Tour for Seniors* https://www.napawineproject.com/how-to-plan-a-memorable-wine-tour-for-seniors/
- *Travel Photography Ultimate Gear Guide 2023* https://theloverspassport.com/travel-photography-gear-guide-2023/
- *A Quick Guide to Starting a Blog as a Senior* https://www.autumnviewgardensellisville.com/blog/a-quick-guide-to-starting-a-blog-as-a-senior

- *Journaling for Seniors: How It Enhances Your Brain Health* https://www.seniorhelpers.com/ca/san-mateo/resources/blogs/journaling-for-seniors-how-it-enhances-your-brain-health/
- *How to share holiday photos with grandparents online* https://www.oscarsenior.com/blog/how-to-share-holiday-photos-with-grandparents-online
- *The 27 Best Travel Gadgets in 2023* https://www.businessinsider.com/guides/tech/best-travel-gadgets
- *Packing Tips for Older Adults* https://www.roadscholar.org/senior-travel-tips/packing-tips/
- *Traveling Abroad with Medicine | Travelers' Health - CDC* https://wwwnc.cdc.gov/travel/page/travel-abroad-with-medicine
- *Top 14 Travel Tips for Seniors [The Complete Travel Guide]* https://blakeford.com/top-14-travel-tips-for-seniors-complete-travel-guide/
- *Special assistance – Travel information* https://www.aa.com/i18n/travel-info/special-assistance/special-assistance.jsp
- *Senior Travel Cards and Discounts* https://seniortravelbuddies.com/senior-travel-cards-and-discounts/
- *International Car Rental Tips You NEED to Know* https://www.smartertravel.com/international-car-rental-tips/
- *Screening for Passengers 75 and Older - Travel - TSA* https://www.tsa.gov/travel/tsa-cares/screening-passengers-75-and-older
- *Senior Travel -How to Find Senior Airfare Discounts* https://www.cheapflights.com/news/how-to-find-senior-airfare-discounts
- *Count the Benefits of Off-Season Travel* https://www.aarp.org/travel/travel-tips/budget/info-2023/off-season-trips.html
- *14 Amazing Free Things To Do for Over-60s in Europe* https://www.starttravel.co.uk/news/10-amazing-free-things-to-do-for-over-60s-in-europe
- *Seniors' Guide to Maximizing Travel Rewards and Discounts* https://goldenlifewiki.com/article/seniors-guide-to-maximizing-travel-rewards-and-discounts
- *Benefits of Group Travel for Older Adults | Road Scholar* https://www.roadscholar.org/senior-travel-tips/benefits-of-group-travel/
- *Sharing Your Story: 10 Ways to Engage Older Adults by Revisiting Memories* https://hummingbirdproject.net/sharing-your-story-10-ways-to-engage-older-adults-by-revisiting-memories/
- *24 Travel Documentaries You Should Watch ASAP* https://www.holidify.com/pages/travel-documentaries-709.html

- *Safe Travel Tips for Older Adults* https://ncoa.org/article/safe-travel-tips-for-older-adults

www.ingramcontent.com/pod-product-compliance
Lightning Source LLC
LaVergne TN
LVHW051835080426
835512LV00018B/2894